Secrets of Tallulah

Histories, Mysteries and Colorful Tales from Tallulah Falls - Georgia's Nineteenth Century Mountain Resort

by Brian A. Boyd

Published by Fern Creek Press • Clayton, Georgia

Secrets of Tallulah

Histories, Mysteries and Colorful Tales from Tallulah Falls - Georgia's Nineteenth Century Mountain Resort

ISBN #1-893651-11-8

Fern Creek Press
P.O. Box 1322
Clayton, Georgia 30525
706.982.3635

"If there are sermons in stones the jagged precipices of Tallulah have preached them to thousands of admirers, to the accompanying of the music of the dashing and foaming waters rushing down from the mountains."

- Athens Weekly Banner, ***March 9, 1906***

Notes of an Early Tourist

In the early 1900s, the Tallulah Falls Railway Passenger Department published a small booklet entitled, "Notes of a Tourist" by Harry Stilwell Edwards. This twelve page booklet contained Edwards' first-hand description of magnificent Tallulah Gorge and the beautiful Blue Ridge region beyond. A few of Mr. Edwards' "notes" are excerpted below to provide a proper introduction to the grandness that is Tallulah:

"A mountaineer, some forty years of age, stood looking down into the grand chasm at Tallulah, speechless with amazement. He maintained silence for some moments after I addressed him, and then said in suppressed tones:

'I reckon you won't want'er b'lieve it, but I was raised in twenty miles of here, an' all my life I been hearin' tell of this place, an'this is the first time I ever came up! I thought the falls was jes' some water tumblin' over the rocks - but - geeminy! I didn't have no idea er whole river was fallin' off a mount'n an' outer sight with a noise like forty thousan' freight trains!'

It was hard to believe, sure enough, but I am satisfied he spoke the truth. Not one percent of the people of Georgia have ever seen Tallulah Falls though within a few hours ride of them, and it is not likely that one percent of the people of the United States have even heard of them. They have been too busy disproving advertisements of lesser attractions at home and abroad.

Tallulah Falls are caused by the Tallulah River, reinforced by Tiger Creek and other tributaries, breaking through the Georgia spur of the Blue Ridge Mountains and descending by a succession of dizzy leaps to the lower lands. It finds its way eventually into the Savannah River and the Atlantic. The sum of these plunges amounts to something like four hundred feet in a single mile, and the force of these waters, estimated at 20,000 horse power, grinding with its arms full of quartz and gravel, can be appreciated only when one looks on the walls of the cliffs, at one place more than seven hundred feet high, and reflects that they once constituted a barrier.

The surrounding scenery is indescribably impressive and beautiful. The sheer cliffs, with their aprons and dadoes of moss and ferns, the spouting springs that send sparkling waters into the canon, the little streams that clamber or leap down to vanish into the mist, the overhanging rocks supporting the weird cedars and lofty pines, constitute an environment that charms every visitor. The wild plunges of the stream - at one point concentrated, at others spread out like a bride's veil - and its ceaseless roar, add a feeling of awe hard to resist. Indeed one is never quite without this feeling more or less defined. The one eternal, unchanging note at Tallulah is a minor, and those who go there for communion find an everlasting atmosphere of solemnity."

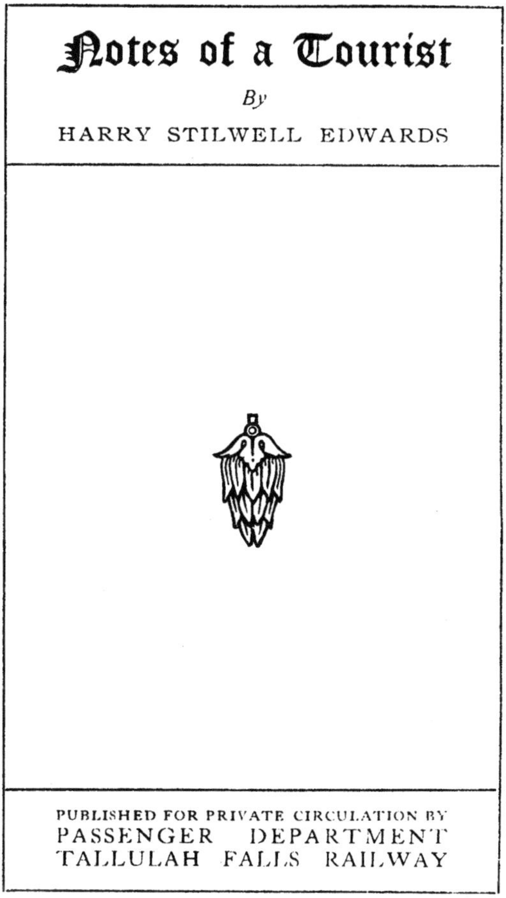

Notes of a Tourist

By

HARRY STILWELL EDWARDS

PUBLISHED FOR PRIVATE CIRCULATION BY
PASSENGER DEPARTMENT
TALLULAH FALLS RAILWAY

Contents

SECRETS of TALLULAH

EARLY HISTORY

THE GLORY YEARS

Introduction

Modern day motorists come upon it suddenly, and many pass by without giving it any thought. From busy U.S. Highway 23/441, the town of Tallulah Falls appears as little more than a random scattering of homes and a few small businesses. Unless you exit the main thoroughfare and venture around the "Old 441" loop, there is little evidence that you are anywhere near one of the most dramatic gorges in eastern North America.

For most who simply pass through, Tallulah Falls is where the rolling hills of the Georgia piedmont become low mountains. Most travelers do not realize however, that this town was once the most highly sought vacation destination in the southern Appalachian region, attracting thousands of visitors each year to an inviting assemblage of upscale hotels, spacious inns and charming boarding houses.

The town of Tallulah Falls is located along the southern rim of the mighty gorge, where the powerful Tallulah River has cut through hundreds of feet of highly resistant quartzite rock over a period of thousands of years. The Tallulah and Tugalo Rivers fall an impressive 1,199 vertical feet along their thirty-nine mile journey from Standing Indian Mountain, located just across the North Carolina line, to the formation of the Savannah River southeast of Tallulah Falls.

Scientists have long speculated on exactly how the gorge was formed. One theory speculates that the Tallulah River was once a part of the Chattahoochee River system, which flows from northeast Georgia southwest through Atlanta. Those who subscribe to this theory believe that the larger Savannah River system to the east eroded upstream at a faster rate, and eventually "captured" the Tallulah River. Proponents of this line of reasoning believe that the gorge was formed over millions of years of persistent erosion.

Modern observations have shown that deep canyons and gorges can form naturally over a relatively short period (geologically speaking), such as those which formed after the Mt. St. Helens eruption in

1980. It seems to reason that the gorge was either carved by a relatively small amount of water (natural river flow) over a long period of time, or by a large amount of water (cataclysmic flood) over a shorter period of time. One thing is for certain - the debate over Tallulah's creation won't end anytime soon.

What remains today is a great geological marvel perched at the very foot of the southern Blue Ridge range. The three-mile long gorge approaches nearly 1,000 feet deep at its deepest point, and its unique combination of highly resistant rock and swift water create some of the most dramatic scenery in the southern Appalachians.

As the town's name implies, there is indeed a waterfall here. In fact, Tallulah Gorge features a full half dozen major waterfalls and just as many smaller cascades which plunge into the gorge from high rocky rims. It is these magnificent natural wonders which have brought notoriety to the gorge, eventually enabling Tallulah Falls to become one of the great upscale resorts and honeymoon destinations in the South. For a brief period of time, extending about one generation, Tallulah Falls was the recreational focal point for the entire region. So great was Tallulah's fame that it eventually became known as the "Niagara of the South."

Though Tallulah Falls experienced rapid growth and great prosperity, a series of events over a period of approximately twenty years almost destroyed the town. In the early 1900s, the Tallulah Falls Railroad was extended northward to Franklin, North Carolina, providing travelers with additional destinations. The next blow to the town occurred in 1913 when the dam at Tallulah Falls was completed, silencing the gorge's famous falls.

In the 1920s, a series of fires destroyed much of Tallulah Falls, including many of the great resort hotels. As a final blow, a modern highway was constructed northward into the southern Blue Ridge in the 1930s, allowing motorists to quickly and conveniently reach points previously unattainable by car. Eventually the town which once hosted the wealthy and powerful became little more than a curiosity along the mighty shoulders of a muted gorge. But as with all curiosities, Tallulah Falls has a great story to share.

Acknowledgments

Much has been written about the colorful history of Tallulah Gorge and Tallulah Falls, and its many fascinating personalities and locations. Because the town's heyday is now nearly a century past, much of its history has faded and become obscured by time. Those who lived through the town's grand resort days have now become a treasured portion of the town's rich legacy. It is with an eye toward helping to preserve their history and their memories that this project has been produced.

It would be nearly impossible to appropriately acknowledge everyone who contributed, either knowingly or unknowingly, to this publication. Undoubtedly, the most extensive research into the town's history was produced by E. Merton Coulter, former Regents Professor of History Emeritus, University of Georgia, and former editor of the *Georgia Historical Quarterly*. Mr. Coulter's *"Tallulah Falls, Georgia's Natural Wonder, From Creation to Destruction"* was featured in the June and September, 1963, issues of the quarterly. His exhaustive research and extensive use of footnotes provided the bulk of information for this publication. Anyone wishing a more detailed study of the town should obtain copies of these excellent articles.

Among the other individuals I am grateful to are Gail DeLoach of the Georgia Department of Archives and History, and Margaret Calhoun of the Georgia Power Company, for their assistance in obtaining many of the photos featured. Thanks to Fred Pitts of Georgia Power Company for historical photos, and to John Kollock for photographs and additional historical background obtained from his writings. Appreciation also goes to Michael Motes, who supplied historical background on several of the personalities featured here, and to John Saye, author of *"The Life and Times of Tallulah...The Falls, The Gorge, The Town."*

I would also like to extend a special word of appreciation to Gae Stovall of Tallulah Gorge State Park for allowing me access to the park's extensive collection of historical material, and for her help with proofing and editing.

Another special word of thanks goes to George and Vickie Prater for use of their extensive collection of original Tallulah Falls postcards. Without them, many of the images contained in this publication would have been absent. Appreciation also goes to Billy Joe Stiles, Rabun Gap-Nacoochee School archivist, for several of the excellent photographs of Aunt Fannie, and George Frizzell, Head of Special Collections at Western Carolina University, for access to the R.A. Romanes collection of photographs.

A word of appreciation is extended to Ted Rowe, for copying *"Notes of A Tourist"* by Harry Stilwell Edwards, so I could provide excerpts for inclusion in this publication. Lastly, a special thanks to Laura Schott for her superb attempt at proofing the mess that I thought was my final draft. So many individuals have graciously assisted in this project that I may have forgotten someone. If so, please accept my heartfelt apology! My sincere gratitude is extended to each of you.

Brian Boyd
January 2003

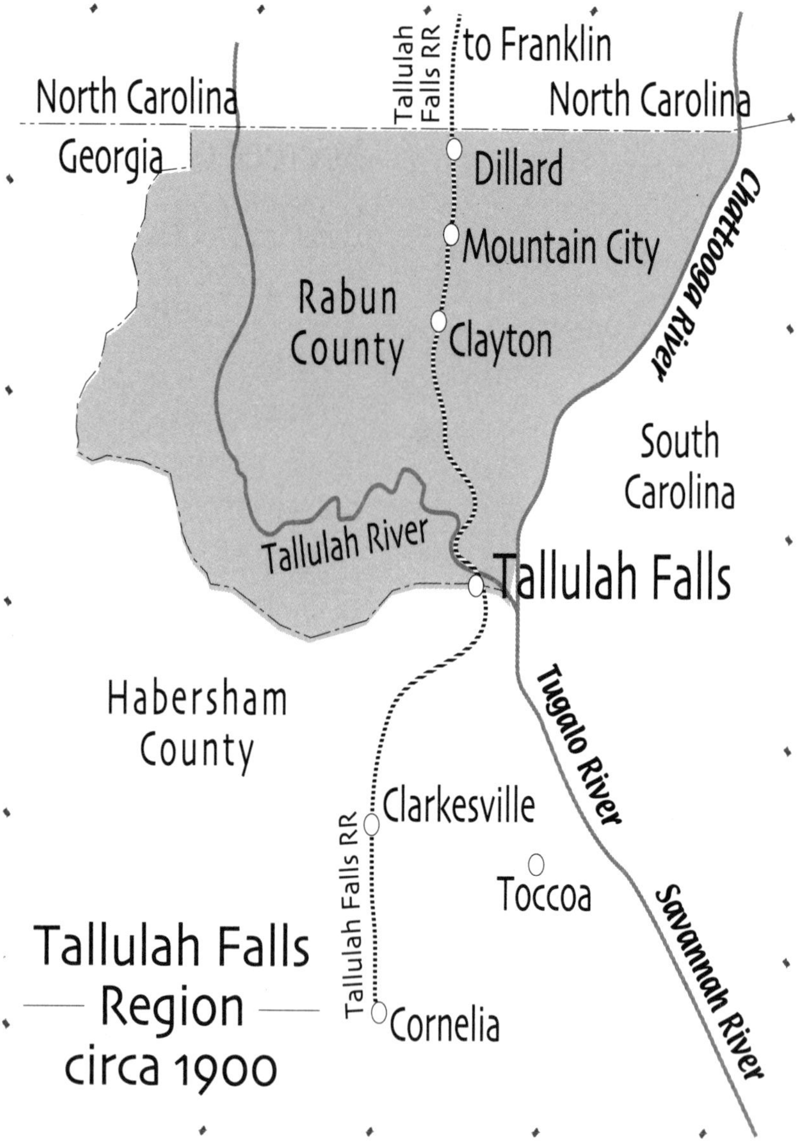
Tallulah Falls RR
to Franklin
North Carolina
North Carolina
Georgia
Dillard
Mountain City
Rabun County
Clayton
Chattooga River
South Carolina
Tallulah River
Tallulah Falls
Habersham County
Tugalo River
Clarkesville
Tallulah Falls RR
Toccoa
Savannah River
Tallulah Falls Region circa 1900
Cornelia

Secrets of Tallulah
EARLY HISTORY
1540 - 1869

Early 1900s postcard view of 76-foot Tempesta Falls.

WHAT'S IN A NAME?
POSSIBLE MEANINGS OF "TALLULAH"

The Cherokee Indians inhabited the Tallulah Falls region long before early white explorers ventured into the rugged southern Appalachians. Though many aspects of their culture remain somewhat mysterious to this day, Cherokee influence on Tallulah Gorge and the immediate region is undeniable. Dozens of area streams and rivers reflect the distinct Cherokee dialect. *"Tallulah"* became the accepted English spelling and pronunciation of the Cherokee name for the awesome gorge and falls, but the true meaning of the term is far from certain. *Tallulah* has been spelled and pronounced a wide variety of ways, including *Talulu, Tellulah, Telulee*, and *Tululah.* Adding to the confusion were several close but slightly different derivatives, including *Tarrurah, Taruri, Terrora, Toruro* and *Turrurar.* Several of these are believed to have been the names of Cherokee settlements along the Tallulah River both above and below the gorge.

By the 1830s, whites sensationalized the translation of *Tallulah* into *"terrible,"* though numerous Cherokee linguists have stated that *Tallulah* cannot be accurately translated. A few experts have even proposed that the true translation could be *"unfinished," "never levels out,"* or perhaps even *"the cry of the frog."*

Adding to the Tallulah mystique, E. Merton Coulter, in an excellent history of Tallulah Falls *(Georgia Historical Quarterly* - June/September 1963), relates that the great-grandparents of the famous actress Tallulah Bankhead visited the falls and were so taken by the grand scenery that they named one of their children Tallulah. The unusual name was eventually passed down through the family and became the name of the famous actress, who proclaimed from her own research that the name may have meant *"love-maiden"* or *"Goddess of Vengeance."*

CHEROKEE LEGENDS - LITTLE PEOPLE, MYSTICAL MAIDENS, & CRAZED LOVERS

It is generally believed that the Cherokee rarely ventured into the foreboding gorge, even to hunt or fish. Rather, they seemed in awe of this imposing cleft in the earth with its sheer cliffs and dramatic waterfalls, which they referred to as "Ugunyl." Several colorful Cherokee myths were told to early white visitors and settlers, further adding to the growing legend of the awesome gorge.

Early Indian stories tell of an unusual race of "little people," called the Yunwi Tsundi, who lived in the caves, crevices and under the waterfalls in Tallulah Gorge. These fierce people were known to kidnap Cherokee women and children and disappear into their hidden strongholds. No Cherokee taken by the little people ever returned, and the cave became known as the entrance to the legendary Happy Hunting Ground. For this reason, the Cherokee avoided the gorge whenever possible. Other versions of this legend contain different details, yet they each paint the little people as hostile and menacing to anyone from the outside world who would dare enter their domain.

Other Cherokee stories tell of mysterious Indian maidens who led an infatuated young warrior to a cave perched high in the sheer gorge walls. A number of supernatural adventures occurred as they traveled to the cave and participated in strange rituals involving turtles, snakes and the brother of one of the maidens. After being warned not to tell anyone of his experience, the young warrior fell into a deep sleep, then awoke in the forest. He could find no trace of the cave or the maidens. The warrior then journeyed back to his own settlement. Those who witnessed his return were astonished. He was told that he had been given up for dead, for he had been missing many years. Ignoring the warning given by the maiden's brother in the cave, the warrior shared his remarkable story with his village. Tragically, he immediately became ill, dying seven days later. Cherokee legend proclaims that no man can betray the secrets of the underworld and live.

Early postcard view of the legendary Cherokee gathering place "Council Rocks," located just above "Lovers' Leap" along the rim of the gorge.

Yet another "legend of Tallulah" related the story of how the high precipice known as "Lovers' Leap" found its name. It seems that many years ago a young white hunter had been captured and was being held prisoner at a Cherokee gathering area known as "Council Rocks." A beautiful Indian maiden by the name of Tallulah was irresistibly drawn to the hunter, and soon fell hopelessly in love with him. Tragically, Tallulah's father sentenced the hunter to be thrown into the gorge from a high cliff just below the Council Rocks. Much to the shock of those who witnessed the execution, the instant the young hunter was thrown over the cliff, the love-stricken maiden leaped after him. From that moment on, the lofty precipice became tragically known as "Lovers' Leap."

"THERE GOES THE NEIGHBORHOOD" EARLY WHITE EXPLORERS AND SETTLERS

Undoubtedly, the first white men to witness the awesome grandeur and raw power of Tallulah Gorge were early explorers. Spaniard Hernando de Soto and his gold-seeking band cut a swath through the southern Appalachians around 1540 and may have visited Tallulah, though no hard evidence confirms this theory. Approximately one hundred-fifty years later, Indian traders pushed into the area. These courageous, self-reliant mountain men may have visited the gorge as early as the late 1600s, perhaps frequenting this magnificent region for nearly two hundred years before the first permanent settlers arrived. Early accounts tell of a traveller who came to Tallulah Gorge in 1821. This visitor reportedly had seen initials and the date *"1718"* carved into several trees in the area.

Relenting to the pressure of white intrusion, the region south of the gorge along the west side of the Tugalo River was obtained through treaties with the Creek and Cherokee Indians in 1783. Franklin County was organized from portions of this territory, as white settlement began to creep ever closer to Tallulah Falls. The lands around the gorge remained under the control of the native Cherokee until the early 1800s. The land west of the Tallulah River was reluctantly ceded by the Cherokee in 1817, followed by the area east of the river in 1819. Habersham County was then formed in 1818, with Rabun County following in 1819.

Settlements in Habersham County obviously developed much more rapidly than Rabun County, primarily due to the gentler terrain and close proximity to rapidly developing towns such as Athens and Gainesville.

In the early 1820s, the village of Clarkesville, initially known as Habersham Court House, was established about twelve miles south of Tallulah Falls. Clarkesville served as the base for most Tallulah visitors from the 1820s through the 1840s, as lodging facilities at the gorge were virtually nonexistent. The only structures in the area were rough, primitive cabins belonging to the earliest settlers.

An early mountain cabin typical of the small, primitive structures built in the Tallulah Falls area in the 1800s. This family appears to be shucking corn. This photo was made by the well-known Tallulah Falls photographer Walter Hunnicutt, courtesy of the Georgia Department of Archives and History.

Early accounts suggest that some of these settlers opened their homes to visitors. An example of this was the Beale House, believed to have been built as early as 1849. Though it often took in guests, the Beale House was little more than a log cabin. Another establishment believed to be a small hotel is rumored to have been operated several miles from the gorge along the Clarkesville Road in the 1850s, but was probably abandoned by the 1860s due to economic hardships involved with the Civil War. By the late 1860s there were probably no public accomodations within five miles of Tallulah Gorge.

The Beale House, one of the Tallulah region's earliest hospitality establishments. Photo courtesy of the Georgia Department of Archives and History.

THE SECRET IS OUT - EARLY DESCRIPTIONS OF THE GREAT GORGE

The early 1800s saw a developing agricultural base in north Georgia, yet the rugged terrain surrounding Tallulah Gorge largely shielded this isolated area. Early hunters and explorers were certainly familiar with the great gorge, but the first published descriptions by a white visitor didn't occur until a September, 1819 article by David Hillhouse appeared in a Milledgeville newspaper, the *Georgia Journal.*

Hillhouse made several treks to Tallulah Gorge that year to explore and map this mysterious chasm. In fact, Hillhouse's estimations concerning the length and depth of the gorge, and the height of many of its falls, were much more accurate than many provided by other early visitors. Hillhouse's article was so well received that it was actually reprinted in a number of other publications through the early and mid-1800s, and became a standard among the many Tallulah Gorge descriptions circulating at that time.

As word of the gorge spread, journalists and visitors alike published a parade of colorful descriptions. Many of these accounts were quite liberal in both descriptive nature and their estimations of Tallulah's dimensions. For example, early "measurements" of the depth of the gorge varied anywhere between 500 feet and 1,500 feet! About the only thing early experts could concur on was that Tallulah Gorge was an area of unusually rare beauty.

Tallulah Gorge did not officially begin to appear on most maps until 1843, when *Darby's Universal Geographical Dictionary* was published in Washington. Ten years later, a description of the falls was also included in the *New and Complete Statistical Gazetteer of the United States.* At last, word of the mysterious chasm had spread across the young republic.

FICTION AT THE FALLS - EARLY WRITERS DISCOVER TALLULAH

Years before the gorge began drawing great crowds of visitors, at least two authors were sufficiently inspired to create works of fiction featuring spectacular Tallulah Gorge as their primary setting. Around 1854, a work entitled *"The Georgia Bequest. Manolia; or, the Vale of Tallulah"* was published. The book was written by William R. Rembert, a self-described wealthy planter of the day.

Rembert's book has been described as a rather disjointed collection of fiction. Merton Coulter's 1963 *Georgia Historical Quarterly* article described the work as a "nondescript hodgepodge work of fiction, in which a beautiful Manolia, a party of University of Georgia students, an old Indian Oothacoochy, and a few other characters played their parts." Rembert's love of the gorge eventually led him to build a summer home near the open, lower end of the gorge sometime after the Civil War.

Ironically, an English-born artist was completing his *second* story set at Tallulah Falls at about the same time Rembert was penning his novel. Twelve years previous, in 1842, T. Addison Richards wrote *"The Trysting Rock: A Tale of Tallulah Falls."* The story appeared in serial form in a locally produced literary magazine, *The Orion: A Monthly Magazine of Literature, Science and Art.* Interestingly, the magazine was published by the author's brother at Penfield, Georgia.

Richards' later novel was entitled *"Kitty, the Woodsman's Daughter."* This, too, stayed in the family, as "Kitty" was published in Richards' own publication, *American Scenery, Illustrated.* The story revolves around a love triangle involving Kitty, a young but shy suitor, David, and a visitor to the falls who happens to save her life when she nearly falls into the raging waters of the gorge. Kitty falls in love with her valiant hero, but attempts suicide by plunging into the river when her affections are not returned. The story ends like all good love stories end, as the smitten David saves his beloved Kitty, and thereby earns her hand in marriage.

PULPITS, THRONES & SQUEEZES - LANDMARKS IN THE GORGE

As the number of visitors to the gorge began to swell, points of particular interest were bestowed proper names. One of the most notable, Devil's Pulpit, was among the easiest to reach and provided one of the most outstanding views of the middle gorge. The pulpit was actually a small protruding ledge perched atop a high, sheer cliff, and soon became a favorite stop of early visitors to the dramatic southern rim. The pulpit provided dramatic views of spectacular Hurricane Falls and a series of rugged cliffs flexing upward to the north rim. Like many features in the gorge, the pulpit was known by a variety of names, including Diana's Rest, the Throne of Aeoleus, and the Student's Rostrum.

Not to be outdone, the north rim also had a favorite overlook - Inspiration Point, or Point Inspiration. Known for its beautiful sunsets, Inspiration Point became a favorite romantic destination. Other notable overlooks along the rim included Lovers' Leap, Deer Leap, Eagle's Nest, Chimney Rock, and Sunset Rock. Trysting Rock, another favorite of those seeking romance, was said to be the location a pair of young Cherokee lovers would meet.

Indian Arrow Rapids was often considered the head of the gorge. Located just below the heart of the town, this was a favorite spot to enjoy a dip in the river. This is the site of present day Tallulah dam.

Top: View of the spectacular Grand Chasm with Angelina Rock in the foreground. Angelina's profile was one of several notable rock formations in and around Tallulah Gorge. From an early postcard.

Bottom: A portion of another early postcard shows infamous Lovers' Leap jutting precariously from a high, sheer cliff. A number of stories have been passed down about how the dangerous precipice gained its name.

The ugly profile of Witch's Head (located in the top right corner of this photograph) was one of the must-see rock formations in the upper gorge. Though slippery and dangerous, the gorge floor from Indian Arrow Rapids to Hawthorne's Pool (including Witch's Head and Ladore Falls) received a great deal of foot traffic due to its close proximity to town and the relatively shallow depth of the gorge at this point. Photo courtesty of the Georgia Department of Archives and History.

The upper gorge "officially" began at Indian Arrow Rapids. Just a stone's throw downstream from these shoals was one of the most interesting rock formations in the gorge. At the base of the gorge on the southern bank of the river, an unmistakeable human profile jutted from a steep rock face just out of reach. This formation became known as Witch's Head, and was reportedly first noticed by a photographer in 1891. High above along the opposite rim, a formation known as Angelina Rock offered a somewhat more attractive profile. Several hundred yards downstream of Witch's Head, beautiful L'Eau d'Or (Ladore) Falls tumbled over a long, sloping ledge. The water stilled momentarily in beautiful Hawthorne's Pool. Rugged Tempesta Falls plunged over a dramatic cliff immediately below the pool, followed by mighty Hurricane Falls a few hundred yards downstream.

The middle gorge, known for its high perpendicular cliffs and imposing forested slopes, featured notable landmarks Oceana Falls, Bridal Veil Falls and Horseshoe Bend. As the name suggests, the river at Horseshoe Bend negotiated a tight 180° bend directly below one of the highest sheer cliffs in the gorge. Below Horseshoe Bend was pretty Sweet Sixteen Falls, the last major drop within the gorge.

Several of the primitive trails traversing Tallulah Gorge featured dramatically narrow passages between rocks or through shallow crevices. One of the most famous of these fissures was Needle's Eye (also known as Lovers' Squeeze), which was located along the trail which descended past the brink of Hurricane Falls upstream to the base of Tempesta. To thread the needle, visitors had to squeeze through a narrow passage between the gorge wall and a huge sloping rock slab. Other notable passages included Giant's Squeeze and Reed's Squeeze.

Clare Hancock and a gentleman identified only as "B.F." strike a dramatic pose atop Inspiration Point, one of the gorge's highest overlooks. Ms. Hancock resided in Tallulah Falls during portions of 1911 and 1912. The caption from her photo album states that this photo was self-taken.

WITHOUT A TRACE? THE MYSTERIOUS DISAPPEARANCE OF REV. HAWTHORNE

One of Tallulah's earliest mysteries involved a drowning in the gorge. This story has been recounted so many times over the decades that the lines separating fact and fiction are largely blurred. The story involves a young man by the name of Hawthorne who was part of a group which visited the gorge on July 5, 1837. Hawthorne was generally believed to have been a Presbyterian minister, though his precise origin is in question. Some recount that he was a native of South Carolina, while others believe that he was from England or Ireland.

Hawthorne is believed to have been part of an Athens group visiting Clarkesville. One account claims that Rev. Hawthorne preached in a local church on Sunday, then left with the group for several days of sightseeing at the gorge. The group followed one of the steep, primitive trails that descended from the south rim to the base of the upper gorge, ending at a beautiful emerald green pool. This pool was nestled at the base of rugged, grey cliffs which stretched several hundred feet high. The pool was positioned directly below a beautiful stairstepping waterfall, and perched directly above yet another dangerous cascade, this one nearly eighty-feet high! After spending the afternoon enjoying the magnificent scene, the group left to take the ladies back out of the gorge to a nearby camping site. Rev. Hawthorne decided to remain in order to enjoy a swim in the clear, cold waters of the beautiful pool.

When his companions returned, Hawthorne had vanished. The only clues his companions were able to locate were his clothes and pocket watch, all placed neatly on a small pine sapling. It was assumed that Hawthorne had been swept out of the pool by the deceivingly strong current and pushed over the dangerous waterfall just downstream. At this point the story becomes even more mysterious.

One version of the story relates that Hawthorne's body was never found, and the cause of death remained in question. Other accounts state that Hawthorne's body was later located downstream and later buried in Clarkesville. Leading further credence to this story, one recollection tells of an old cemetery in Clarkesville which featured a large, overgrown grave marker with the initials "F. W. H.." The marker is said to have contained no other information. To this day, there are some who believe this to be the final resting place of young Hawthorne.

The tragic mystery of Hawthorne's disappearance and death may never be completely solved, though his place in the legend and lore of Tallulah Gorge is secure. The pool in which Hawthorne supposedly enjoyed his final swim now bears his name, as does one of the cascades which plunges down the rugged cliffs to the boulder-studded floor of the gorge.

In addition, the pine sapling which is said to have held Hawthorne's clothes and watch was for many years referred to as the Hawthorne Pine.

Modern-day guests who visit the park's dramatic north rim overlooks high above Hawthorne's Pool may wish to pause and remember the young minister who tragically met his Maker at this very spot over one hundred-fifty years ago.

Beautiful Hawthorne's Pool and the rugged cliffs below the north rim.

ESQUIRES AND GRINDSTONES - EARLY SETTLERS AND COLORFUL CHARACTERS

Among the first white settlers into the Tallulah Falls region was a man named Adam Vandevere. Vandevere went by several names, among them "Esquire Vandevere" and the "Hunter of Tallulah." Vandevere reportedly obtained his land initially by trading with the local Indians, but obtained legal claim to over 100 acres at the lower end of the gorge near the junction of the Tallulah and Chattooga Rivers by the 1840s, though possibly as early as the 1820s. Here, at this wildly isolated spot, Vandevere built a small log cabin.

Esquire Vandevere, described as a small man with a long white beard and narrow face, was legendary for his story-telling abilities, and reportedly enjoyed retelling his adventures and accomplishments fighting the Indians in the Creek War. Vandevere was also famous for his hunting exploits, once telling of wrestling a buck deer on the edge of the gorge. As the story goes, both man and animal fell into the river, but each miraculously lived to duel again. Vandevere was prolific in other areas as well, as he reportedly had at least three wives, and boasted of fathering over thirty children. Vandevere is said to have lived at the gorge until the late 1860s, when he was believed to have been well into his eighties.

Sometime before the War Between the States, a man named Weaver lived in the vicinity of the falls. Known as "Old Grindstone," Mr. Weaver boasted of discovering a huge chunk of gold in a cave deep within the gorge. The huge piece of gold was supposedly as big as a grindstone, hence the name. Tragically for Old Grindstone, the priceless gold mysteriously disappeared. Apparently, Mr. Weaver enjoyed the same reputation for tall tales as Adam Vandevere, also boasting of his prolific hunting abilities.

I NEED MY SPACE - HERMITS MAKE TALLULAH THEIR HOME

Some of the most interesting and enigmatic personalities to inhabit the Tallulah Falls region included several hermits who made the gorge their home. The first was probably John Cole Vandevere, who lived in a log cabin near the upper end of the gorge in the mid-1860s. As one would expect, Cole was a near recluse, reportedly associating with no one except his father, Esquire Vandevere.

Differing descriptions of John Cole led some to believe that there were actually two men. One was described as an "aged hunter and trapper," the other as being in his mid-twenties with shoulder-length hair. Though little else is known of this individual(s), at least one of the men was believed to have mysteriously disappeared from the area sometime around 1869.

Other hermits who made Tallulah their home included a Mr. Ledford, who is believed to have inhabited the gorge from the early 1920s through the early 1940s. Incredibly, Mr. Ledford lived in a shallow cave set along the rugged gorge rim. Ledford is said to have seldom left his adopted home, but one exception was immediately after the bombing of Pearl Harbor in 1941. Though it was believed he was in his sixties at the time, the story goes that he went to town in order to register for the draft.

The enigmatic Ledford was described as having a long, silver beard, and (unlike Adam Vandevere) is said to have been afraid of women. It is believed that Ledford decided to live a life of relative solitude after an ugly family squabble left him an outcast.

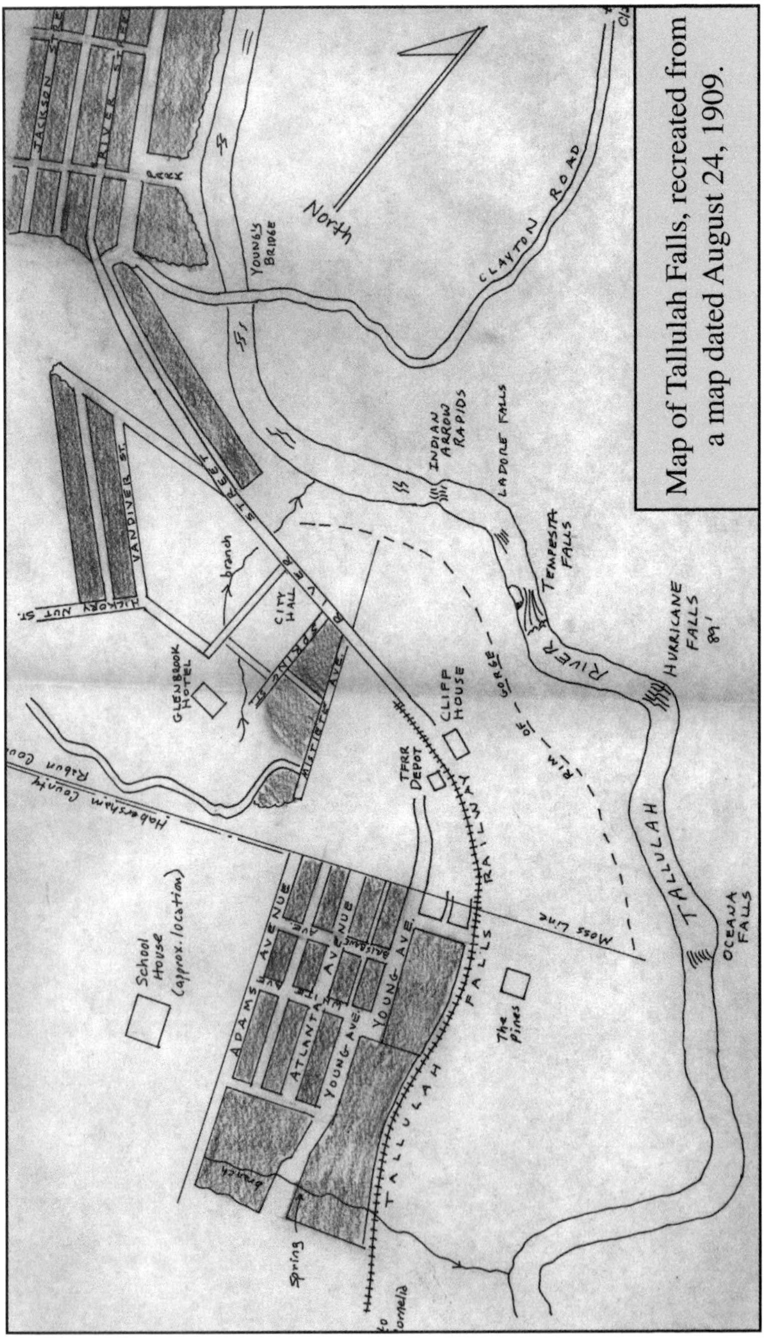

Map of Tallulah Falls, recreated from a map dated August 24, 1909.

Secrets of Tallulah
THE GLORY YEARS
1870 - 1913

IT'S OFFICIAL - TALLULAH FALLS BECOMES A TOWN

Once the earliest descriptions were published and circulated, word of the marvelous gorge at the foot of the Blue Ridge began to spread far and wide. Within just a few short years, the hundreds of visitors who were journeying to the gorge each year quickly grew into the thousands.

Around 1870, James P. Shirley built the first of many "modern" accommodations in the Tallulah Gorge area. The Shirley Hotel was located on the Clarkesville Road just over a mile from the gorge. Business must have been brisk, as Shirley reportedly announced an expansion of the hotel in 1871. The small community of Shirley Grove today stands near the site of Shirley's establishment.

Visitors began to stream into the area in larger numbers, and not just for the spectacular scenery. Hunters and fishermen came to Tallulah to enjoy unspoiled wilderness sporting opportunities. A number of estab-

The stately Cliff House Hotel stood across from the railroad depot on the main thoroughfare through town. Note the speed limit sign (10 mph) hanging overhead. Photo circa early 1920s.

Wiley Pitts, Tallulah Falls mail carrier, unloads a bag of mail from the train at the Tallulah Falls depot, circa 1911. Courtesy of the Georgia Department of Archives and History.

lishments were begun in the 1870s which offered guide services into the area's abundant forests. Prices varied, but were generally around $1.50 per day and $25.00 per month. By 1877, estimates were that nearly 2,000 visitors made the difficult journey to witness the wonders of the mighty gorge and falls.

Tallulah Falls was well established as a booming tourist destination by the time it was officially organized into a town in 1885. At this time, around 100 individuals called Tallulah Falls home. Citizens serving as commissioners at that time were R.L. Moss, Tom Robinson, J.M. Cartledge and William Berry. By 1889, the town of Tallulah Falls was incorporated, extending the city limits one-half mile in each direction.

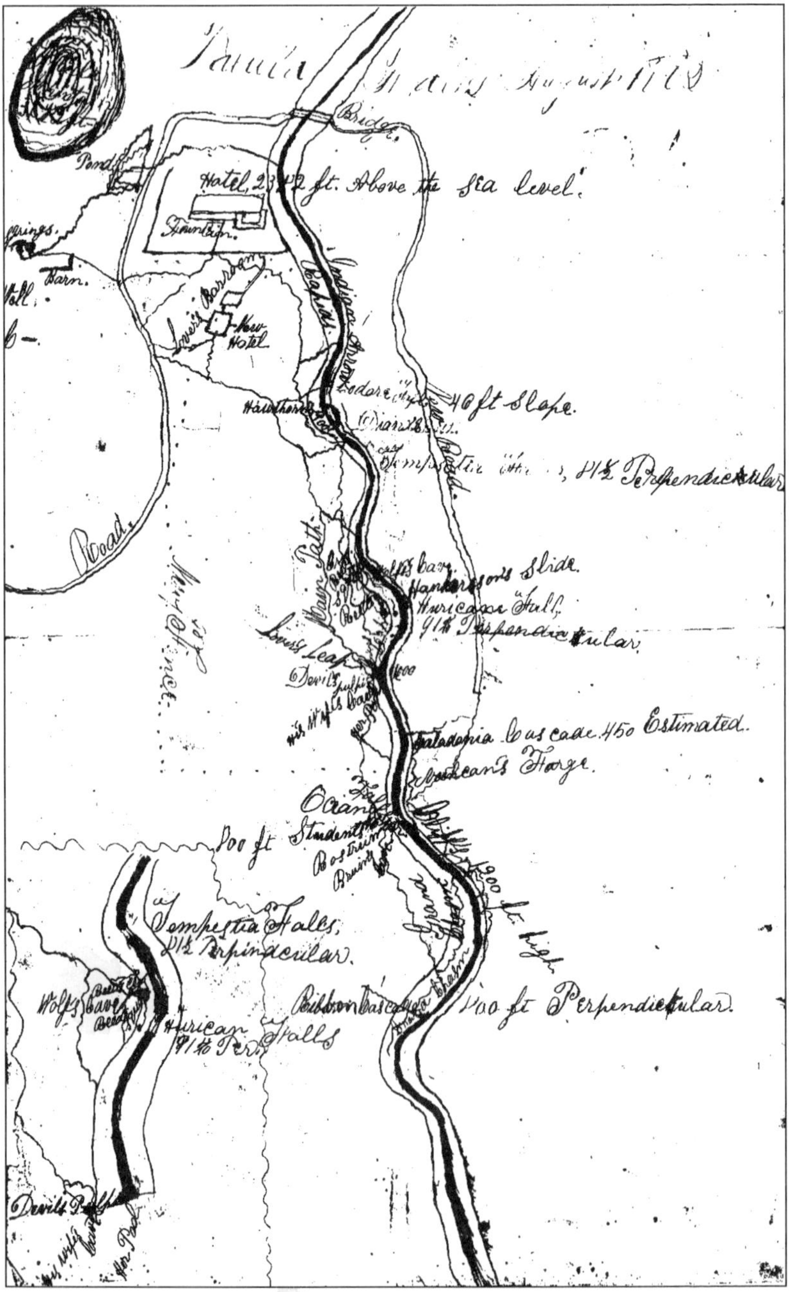

Copy of a hand-drawn map of the gorge and town believed to be from 1879.

"HEY BUDDY, YOU CAN'T PARK THAT MULE HERE" MAINTAINING ORDER IN THE TOWN

In its early years, Tallulah Falls was wild and isolated - somewhat of a frontier town. But just like in the wild West, one did not want to run afoul of the law. To aid in keeping the peace and maintaining a certain degree of civilization, the town enforced a series of ordinances. The following are just a few which were adopted February 1, 1890.

TOWN ORDINANCES

Sec. 16th. No horse, mule or ass shall run loose in any street, sidewalk or alley in the town of Tallulah Falls, nor shall any beast of burden or any animal be hitched to any shade tree, fence post, lamp post, or telegraph post in town. Any person found guilty of this offense shall pay a fine not exceeding ten dollars.

Sec. 25th. All idle, mischievous and disorderly persons shall be arrested, and if found guilty shall work on the streets or be confined in the calaboose at the discretion of the mayor.

Sec. 26th. All suspicious characters found loitering about or within the said town shall be arrested and ordered to leave town. Any person so notified and refusing to obey shall be dealt with as prescribed in the state vagrancy law.

Sec. 52nd. It shall be the duty of the Marshall to be at the depot at the departure and arrival of all trains from the first of June to the first of October, and to see that peace and perfect order are preserved, and that no one jump on or off said train while in motion unless he be an employee of said road or passenger leaving. And to keep each and every one a distance of six feet from said train until the passengers get off unless he is there to meet a friend or helping off the same.

"SHE'LL BE COMING AROUND THE MOUNTAIN!" THE ARRIVAL OF THE RAILROAD

Undoubtedly, the single greatest factor in Tallulah Falls' explosive growth during the late 1800s was the arrival of the railroad. In 1854, the Georgia General Assembly passed an act calling for the development of a rail line from Athens to Clayton. Seventeen years later, in 1871, construction of a line from Cornelia to Tallulah Falls was begun by the North Eastern Railroad, which was subsequently bought out by the Richmond & Danville System around 1881. The line reached the budding town of Tallulah Falls in 1882, fueling an explosion of tourism and development.

In 1887, the Richmond & Danville sold the line to the Blue Ridge and Atlantic Railroad Company. The BR&A had plans to utilize this segment to complete a rail line from Savannah, GA, to Knoxville, TN, but poor financial conditions forced the company into receivership for

A long passenger train pausing in Tallulah Falls around 1910 or 1911. Note the early depot on the right, and the front porch of the Cliff House on the left.

The railroad's open-air "Executive Car" circa 1917. Photo courtesy of the Georgia Department of Archives and History.

five years. In 1898, the Tallulah Falls Railway Company was formed and purchased the twenty-one mile segment from Cornelia to Tallulah Falls. Soon afterwards, construction resumed northward toward the isolated town of Clayton about a dozen miles north. By 1904, the Tallulah Falls Railroad reached Clayton, and was soon afterwards extended to its northern terminus of Franklin, NC, by 1907.

THE RAILROAD AND THE TOWN

The railroad provided the absolute pinnacle in upscale transportation in the late 1880s. While previous visitors to the gorge were forced to make the journey on foot, horseback, or in wagons along muddy, bumpy, primitive roads, the railroad offered the irresistible combination of speed, comfort and affordability. Weekend excursion trains ran from both Atlanta and Athens, costing $3.35 and $2.50 per person, respectively. The final leg of the trip involved a one hour-fifteen minute ride from Cornelia which featured Habersham's picturesque rolling hills and several dra-

Above: Classic postcard view shows a passenger train near Tallulah Falls in the late 1800s. Below: An 1891 Blue Ridge & Atlantic Railroad timetable.

Blue Ridge & Atlantic R. R

Time Table No. 1.

In effect February 1, 1891.

9	11		12	10
Daily	Sat. Only	STATIONS	Daily	Only
a m	p m	Leave / Arrive	a m	p m
6 20	7 50	Tallulah Falls	12 25	10 55
6 3	8 05	Turnerville	12 05	10 40
6 52	8 20	Anandale	11 45	10 25
7 15	8 30	Clarkesville	11 8	10 15
7 30	8 45	Demorest	11 20	10 00
7 45	9 00	Cornelia	11 05	9 45
		Arrive / Leave		

W. B. Thomas,
President and General Manager.

matic wooden trestle crossings. Those who had been previously unable to witness Tallulah's wonders could now step from a modern passenger train just a short walk from the dramatic gorge rim.

For over twenty years, Tallulah Falls was the final stopping point along the line. A large turntable located below the depot turned the locomotive in the opposite direction for its return trip south. Though an extension of the line northward was highly desired, the rugged terrain north of Tallulah Falls stopped construction until the needed capital could be raised. Around the turn of the century, a long, dramatic trestle was constructed just west of the depot which extended out over the rooftops of Tallulah Falls, providing dramatic evidence of the push northward.

A series of depots built directly across the tracks from the famous Cliff House Hotel became the social center of town. Large crowds assembled each day to greet incoming trains, and passengers arriving in the busy summer months were often serenaded by one of several bands employed by the larger hotels. One of the first depots was a charming two-story wooden structure painted red, with white trim bordering the

View of the rugged Tallulah River above the town of Tallulah Falls. This view is from the original wooden truss bridge spanning the river. Photo courtesy of the Georgia Department of Archives and History.

In its latter years, the railroad was reduced to the role of hauling freight. This 1946 photo shows a steam locomotive pulling a string of northbound freight cars across Tallulah Lake.

windows and cornerboards. This structure burned in the early 1900s, but was soon replaced by a beautiful new depot featuring a distinctive red-tile roof. Ironically, though the railroad and most of the town's historic structures were destroyed or fell into disrepair decades ago, the last of the Tallulah Falls Railway's depots survives remarkably sound into the twenty-first century.

The railroad was a prime spot for photographs in the early years of the town. In fact, many of the photographic images which offer us bits and pieces of how the town actually looked at the dawn of the twentieth century were taken by those photographing some aspect of the railroad.

NO PETS ALLOWED - THE GRAND HOTEL ERA: 1882 - 1912

With the advent of the railroad in 1882, a flood of visitors poured into Tallulah Falls. Entrepreneurs and businessmen quickly envisioned the need for upscale hotels and inns to meet the demand of increasing tourism. Soon afterwards began a building boom which changed the town dramatically, inaugurating the period known as the Grand Hotel Era.

YOUNG'S HOTEL

One of the original principal players in the development of the Tallulah Falls hotel business was W. D. Young and family. Young built the Young's Hotel, also known as the Tallulah Hotel, sometime around 1876. This establishment was located on the brink of the upper gorge just above beautiful Indian Arrow Rapids, a favorite bathing spot. Young's Hotel burned in 1885 or 1886, but was quickly rebuilt, as its prime location made it a favorite boarding choice.

A great many visitors and part-time Tallulah Falls residents came from nearby Athens, a mere sixty miles to the south. Because of this, items of interest and advertisements covering Tallulah Falls often appeared in Athens' newspapers. The following two items concerning Young's Hotel appeared in the same edition of an 1885 newspaper:

Tallulah Topics - *The Banner-Watchman*, August 5, 1885

The Visitors

There are now about 300 guests at the falls. We stopped at Young's Hotel, and found it well filled. He has a fine band on hand, and there is dancing every night. It is a gay place, and a number of lovely ladies are now his guests. Mr. and Mrs. Young are great popular favorites with the traveling public, and do all in their power to make the visitors have a nice time.

Advertisement - *The Banner-Watchman*, August 5, 1885

YOUNG'S HOTEL - Tallulah Falls, Georgia

This hotel overlooks the Grand Rapids and commands a fine view of the river, and is located in North-East Georgia, on the south slope of the Blue Ridge, and has a delightful climate, being 2,000 feet above the sea; highest temperature 92 degrees. The nights are cool and refreshing. The Hotel has 3,000 feet of verandah and 100 rooms, and is supplied with the best freestones from the mountains. There are also mineral springs of fine medicinal qualities - iron, saltpeter and magnesia - within two hundred yards of the hotel.

The scenery about the falls and in view of the hotel is as sublime and enchanting as any mountain scenery in the world. Five beautiful falls dash their water in piles of snowy whiteness down 450 feet of rocks within less than half a mile. Every turn in the precipeses path along the side of the gorge through which the Tallulah River flows discloses new pictures of sublimity and beauty. One can stand on the brink of this rushing current and look up at pines and firs which have their roots placed on the edge of the rocky cliff 1,000 feet overhead. Fountains and springs surprise one on every side. The soft strains of music soothe one to slumber at night. The roaring of the cataract sounds a pleasant lullaby to make sleep secure.

For those who wish cool nights for sleep, or who, lithe of limb and full of sound of lung, like to climb precipices and romp over mountains by day, this is the place for them, especially if they be slender of purse or have an eye to economy.

There are Billiards and Cards, Horses and Carriages, Tenpins and Dancing, and Deer, Turkey, Squirrels and Quail for those sportively inclined. Depot and Telegraph office within 200 yards of the hotel. Trains arrive and leave daily making close connections with trains on Air Line railroad at Rabun Gap Junction.

Terms of Board

$3 per day, $10 per week, $30 to $40 per month. Special rates made with family. Servants $16 per month. For further information apply to

W.D. Young
Owner and Proprietor

THE GRAND VIEW

Several hundred yards east of Young's Hotel was another Young family enterprise, the impressive Grand View Hotel. Located just above the railroad on a gentle rise, this structure was the first of Tallulah Falls' classic Victorian structures. Its ornate, two-story design featured a large cupola on the roof. An expansive park was said to have extended from the front of the hotel to the brink of the south rim, with a number of lofty observation points offering dramatic views of the middle gorge.

The Grand View was known for its popular mineral springs, which were said to impart great physical benefits. In addition, a large bathing pool proved quite popular during the sweltering summer months. The Grand View opened in 1886 with much fanfare as it hosted Professor Leon, famed aerialist who was in Tallulah Falls to perform a daring high wire walk across the gorge.

In the early 1890s Mr. Young faced a pleasant difficulty - his hotel was frequently filled to capacity. He subsequently built the Willard House about 100 yards to rear of the Grand View. The two were reportedly connected by a long, covered walkway. Unfortunately, the stately Grand View was destroyed by fire on June 29, 1897, having stood as a Tallulah Falls landmark for just a little over one short decade. An article in the *Tallulah Falls Spray* stated the value of the hotel at $15,000 to $20,000, but insurance coverage was listed at only $8,000.

THE CLIFF HOUSE

The largest of the grand Tallulah Falls hotels was the Cliff House. Built in 1882 by the Moss family from Athens, the grounds of the Cliff House covered forty spacious acres. The hotel adopted its name from San Francisco's legendary Cliff House, which offered a dramatic panorama of the rocky Pacific Coast. It seems that Mr. Moss had taken his new bride west for a California honeymoon. He was so impressed with San Francisco's famous Cliff House that he boasted of building one of his own back in Georgia. The Tallulah Falls version was located directly across the railroad tracks from the depot, and quickly became a social

A longer range view of the Cliff House from well across the railroad tracks.

center of Tallulah Falls.

The original structure had over ninety rooms (later expanded to one hundred forty rooms) and could accommodate over 300 guests. Its expansive dining room could seat over 250. The Cliff House was quite

Early twentieth century visitors gather on the spacious front porch of the Cliff House. Photo courtesy of the Georgia Department of Archives and History.

close to many of the more popular hiking destinations, as it was located along the upper gorge in the vicinity of the famous Witch's Head and Devil's Pulpit rock formations. Additional activities included lawn tennis, bowling, billiards, ping-pong, and card playing.

A large band from Athens spent the summers playing here in exchange for free room and board. As such, the many varied sounds of late nineteenth century music were commonplace in the hotel and throughout the grounds.

Another view of the impressive front porch at the Cliff House. This photo was taken from a point adjacent to the railroad depot.

Though the Cliff House survived a tragic 1921 fire which destroyed much of the town of Tallulah Falls, it too finally succumbed to flames in 1937. The fire which destroyed the Cliff House is said to have been started by sparks from a passing train. If this is true, it is fitting, as it was the railroad which enabled Tallulah Falls to become a prime tourist destination in the first place.

TALLULAH LODGE

Located along the railroad at the line's highest point of elevation between Cornelia and Tallulah Falls, beautiful Tallulah Lodge was about one mile southeast of "downtown" Tallulah Falls. This massive two-story, solid white Colonial structure was built in the 1890s in an area known as Tallulah Park. Early publications described the lodge as one of the finest hotels in the region, and as such it catered primarily to the wealthy and well-to-do. Rates for the lodge were $2 (and up) per day, $10 - $17 per week.

Stately Tallulah Lodge circa 1911.

Everything about this beautiful structure was absolutely first class. Patrons passed between four stately columns before entering the lodge's massive two-story lobby, which featured rich carpet, white willow chairs and a massive stone fireplace. An exclusive ladies' parlor was located on the eastern end of the lobby. The lodge boasted over 150 rooms and could accommodate over 250 guests. Fifty of these rooms featured private baths, which was at that time considered a luxury.

The grand two-story entrance lobby was the focal point for social gatherings at upscale Tallulah Lodge.

The lodge featured well tailored, expansive grounds which extended to the highest rims of the gorge and included an overlook known as Paradise Point. From this lofty perch, patrons enjoyed dramatic views into the eastern end of the gorge, as well as of the high mountains to the north extending well into North Carolina.

In the summer months an orchestra further added to the upscale setting. For those who wished for other forms of recreation, tennis, tenpins, horseback riding, card parties and dancing were among the favorite activities. Patrons desiring to visit Tallulah Falls proper could ride down into town on a canopied railroad flatcar. This trip took riders along the dramatic southern rim of the gorge, including a transit of the lofty Pine Pole trestle.

In its final years, the Georgia Railway and Power Company utilized the lodge during construction of the North Georgia Hydro Project. Though hotel literature claimed a fire protection system, Tallulah Lodge continued an infamous tradition of famous Tallulah Falls hotels, as it too was destroyed by fire, in 1916.

BOARDING HOUSES & COTTAGES

A number of popular boarding houses, inns and "cottages" operated in Tallulah Falls during the late 1800s and early 1900s. Most of these accommodated only a few dozen guests. Among the more intimate accommodations were The Pines, Buena Vista, Taylor House, Maplewood Inn, Garson House, Moody House, Moore House, Moss House, Rocky Bottom, Willard House, Robinson House, and Glenbrook Cottage.

ROBINSON HOUSE

The Robinson House, run by T. A. Robinson, was located on the gorge rim just above Indian Arrow Rapids. The Robinson House was reportedly converted from a skating rink in 1885, and enjoyed an excellent reputation for its hospitality and dining. The following write-up appeared in the "Tallulah Topics" section of the Athens newspaper *The Banner-Watchman* on August 5, 1885:

> Mr. T. A. Robinson
>
> Gentle readers, one of the Seven Wonders of Tallulah Falls is Tom Robinson. He is a brick, and a gold brick at that. Mr. Robinson started life at a very early age, without a stitch of clothing on his back or a dollar in his pocket. From this small beginning, Robinson has rapidly climbed up the ladder of fortune until he today is the proud owner of a skating rink, a grey mule, a soda fountain and a blue flannel shirt. Mr. R. has a heart as large as Stone Mountain. He will turn himself wrong side out any time for a friend. Tom Robinson made a mash on us last Sunday, and we are now getting up an excursion party from Athens just to see him.

Mr. Robinson was evidently quite the busy fellow, as he reportedly also ran one of the local bars (which was rumored to have done a tremendous business) and found time to serve a stint as mayor in the town's boisterous early years.

WILLARD HOUSE

Built in the 1890s by the Young family, the Willard House, or Willard Cottage, stood proudly on a low hill overlooking the railroad on the corner of Young and White Avenues. Named for Mrs. Francis E. Willard, its steep facade, featuring three gabled dormers and a large front porch, proudly faced the south rim of the gorge. The inn was once reportedly connected to the famed Grand View Hotel via a 100-yard long, covered walkway, though the latter burned in 1897. The Willard House accommodated about 75 guests, and remained in operation through much of the early 1900s.

The stately Willard House lies under a shallow blanket of winter snow. This is the view of the hotel from the approximate location of the Tallulah Falls Railroad line.

GLENBROOK COTTAGE

The Glenbrook Cottage was among the best known of the cottages in town, perhaps because it was operated well past the time when Tallulah Falls' other hotels closed down. The Glenbrook survived intact well into the late 1900s, long after the other structures had burned or been torn down, and its memory accordingly lingers on.

The Glenbrook's location and design were among its main attractions. The cottage was located above the town just a short walk from the

A group of staff and guests pose in front of the original Glenbrook Cottage.

railroad depot. The front of the main building featured a delightful montage of roof lines - towers, dormers, gables. On the grounds were springs, a small pool, gazebos and picnic spots. Not to be outdone, the Glenbrook's dining accommodations were highly praised. The Glenbrook later underwent a large addition which added a multi-storied side wing onto its original structure, greatly increasing its capacity.

Those who remember the Glenbrook often recall its beautiful appointments, including a large front lobby with an ornate wooden floor and intricate scrollwork. The hotel was constructed on a dizzying array of levels, and many of the windows in the cottage featured imported stained glass. Reportedly filled with costly pictures, photographs and engravings, the Glenbrook had a fascinating aura surrounding it. The cottage boasted of a popular honeymoon suite which evidently did quite a bit of business.

Built around 1894 as a private residence for Dr. Percy Trant Hickson Norcop, the Glenbrook was reportedly enlarged around 1897. Business steadily decreased after 1913, but it managed to remain in operation

This group poses for a photographer along the edge of a small pool on the front lawn of the Glenbrook.

until the early 1940s. The hotel opened again for a limited run in the 1950s, but by this time the hospitality business was largely unprofitable in Tallulah Falls.

Today, the once magnificent Glenbrook Cottage is a rotting corpse, a faint shadow of its previous opulence. The rapidly deteriorating structure is still visible just above the town of Tallulah Falls in the cold, leafless winter months. Interested parties would be well-advised to resist the temptation to visit its ruins, as portions of the structure have collapsed. This once proud final survivor from Tallulah Falls' proud past has been left to die abandoned, forlorn and disgraced.

BOYS WILL BE BOYS - TROUBLE IN PARADISE

With Tallulah's abundant beauty and an ever-increasing flood of visitors, one might assume that life at the Falls was always enchanting and free of conflict. Unfortunately, since the day mankind was kicked out of the garden there have been squabbles and disagreements.

During the frenzied 1880s, competing interests worked feverishly to develop attractive hotels and inns. Naturally, competition was keen, which sometimes led to the brink of outright conflict. The following article appeared in *The Banner-Watchman* (Athens, GA) in 1885:

TALLULAH TROUBLES

From parties just returned from this popular resort, we learn that there is considerable trouble between Mr. R. L. Moss, proprietor of one hotel, and Mr. Young, proprietor of the other. Mr. Young owns the springs around the falls, and Mr. Moss owns most of the falls. Mr. Moss wanted Mr. Young to allow him to run a pipe to the spring to bring water to his hotel and cottages. Mr. Young agreed to give him water privileges for one dollar per day. Mr. Moss, thinking this charge too much, and as he owned most of the beautiful scenery, told Mr. Young he would allow his guests to go through his land and view the falls for the water privileges. This Young refused to do, and Moss fenced up all of his land, thereby cutting off visitors stopping at Young's Motel from viewing the sights unless they would pay .25 cents for admission through the gate. The war still wages and we may look for some rich developments. Mr. Moss has nearly completed his fence, while Young is well fortified about the springs. We hope this trouble may be settled, as the water and beautiful scenery should be free to all.

History isn't exactly clear on how the two men managed to solve the problem, but the August 5, 1885 edition of *The Banner-Watchman* reported on the cooling of hostilities:

MOSS VS. YOUNG

> With the exception of a plank barricade in front of Young's hotel, all signs of the late conflict is over. Mr. Moss makes no charge for using his grounds, neither does Mr. Young. The only inconvenience is that Young's guests have to go up to the gate, at the depot, to pass in. Next winter Mr. Young will build a bridge across the river opposite his hotel, make a good path on the other side of the chasm, and he will then be as independent as a wood sawyer.

In spite of the differences which inevitably arose, those who ran establishments in Tallulah Falls knew they were in the hospitality business. Even if they could not get along with one another, they had an excellent reputation for showing their many visitors a grand time. In the case of Moss vs. Young, it appears neither was willing to battle the other at the expense of their own bottom line. We can only look back and suppose that each was willing to let bygones be bygones.

BORN TO RUN - THE MIGHTY FALLS OF THE TALLULAH

Before the construction of Tallulah dam, the Tallulah River flowed freely past the town's River Street. The riverbed was approximately one hundred feet below the gorge rim near the lower end of town. Here the swift current plunged over a series of small drops known as Indian Arrow Rapids. Visitors would often come here to swim, sun, or explore the many pools and potholes in this area.

The four major waterfalls for which Tallulah Falls was renowned all occured downstream over the next half mile in the rugged heart of Tallulah Gorge. The first drop was just a few hundred yards below Indian Arrow Rapids. Known as L'Eau d'Or (Ladore) because the sunlight on its shimmering water often resembled gold, this long, crashing 50-foot drop stilled briefly in magnificent, emerald-green Hawthorne's Pool. Nestled at the base of a rugged rocky cliff reaching over 100 feet toward the sky,

A group of high school students admire the rugged beauty of Ladore Falls sometime around 1900. Courtesy of the Georgia Department of Archives and History.

Hawthorne's Pool was the site of a tragic drowning in 1837.

Below Hawthorne's Pool, the thundering echo of yet more crashing water and rising clouds of mist alerted visitors to the next Tallulah treasure, beautiful 76-foot Tempesta Falls. This aptly named waterfall tumbles in a narrow, fluming cascade over a sheer rocky cliff. The magnificent Cliff House built a series of boardwalks along the cliffs which led to a five-story observation tower overlooking Tempesta.

Powerful 76-foot Tempesta plunges from tranquil Hawthorne's Pool. Photo courtesy of the Georgia Power Corporate Archives.

A short walk downstream, the river was hemmed in by two towering rock cliffs. As the river surged between the two, it plummeted over mighty 96-foot Hurricane Falls. Tallulah's highest and most awesome cataract, Hurricane received its name for the deafening sound the water produced as it roared over the cliff. The area around Hurricane was extremely dangerous, as the rocks along the brink were treacherously slippery. Those at the base were even worse, as they were perpetually soaked by clouds of drenching spray. The trail from the brink to the base was extremely steep, and visitors who wished to make the steep descent were forced to utilize primitive boardwalks and cables. Those who endured were rewarded with a breathtaking site as the Tallulah River exploded over Hurricane in a frenzy of deafening whitewater.

The awesome scene at Hurricane Falls during a flood in 1911 or 1912. Note the tremendous cloud of spray from the waterfall.

A broad pool stilled the river momentarily below Hurricane, a stark contrast to the whitewater carnage just above. A small portion of Hurricane Falls spilled into a small, separate pool just above the main plunge pool, treacherously positioned between Hurricane and a steep cliff. At low water levels this water became trapped, often becoming stagnant or brackish, and thus received the name Devil's Foot Bath.

The fourth major waterfall occurred several hundred yards downstream. Broad, fifty-foot Oceana brought to mind mighty foam-capped waves which might be found at the seaside. Unlike the other large falls, Oceana was extremely broad, as the Tallulah's waters spread out to rush over a massive sloping ledge. Because of all the tremendous scenery found in such a small area, this portion of the gorge became known as the Grand Chasm.

Top: Rare postcard of Sweet Sixteen Falls, the last of the major waterfalls in Tallulah Gorge. Sweet Sixteen is probably the least photographed of the major waterfalls due to its remote location.

Bottom: Vintage postcard shows a wide angle view of Ladore Falls in the western, upper end of the gorge. Compare with the photo back on page 42 for perspective.

Above: The massive 50-foot wall of water known as Oceana Falls, as pictured on a vintage postcard from the early 20th century.

Below: An early postcard accurately captures Bridal Veil's graceful appearance. Note that the postcard lists Bridal Veil as 37 feet high, though actually its height is closer to 20 feet. Compare with photo on page 99.

Below Oceana the river rushed among a maze of boulders and over dozens of small shoals. Ahead, several treasures awaited - among them, beautiful Bridal Veil Falls. Estimated at about 20 feet, Bridal Veil was formed where the Tallulah River gracefully dispersed over a massive, gently sloping ledge, its waters sliding headlong into a broad plunge pool. The gentle slope produced thin, intricate waves of white-veiled water, hence the name.

Below Bridal Veil, the river surged through dramatic Horseshoe Bend at the base of one of Tallulah Gorge's highest sheer cliffs. Downstream, the last of the Tallulah's notable falls, Sweet Sixteen, provided a fitting climax to the assemblage of mighty falls.

Like all of Tallulah's falls, Sweet Sixteen was quite beautiful, but was fairly far from the major hotels of the day, near the deepest portion of the gorge. Any hiking excursions reaching this point would take a good bit of the day and a great amount of stamina.

In addition to the major waterfalls, several feeder creeks plunged from the rim to the river via cascades ranging anywhere from 150 feet to nearly 1,000 feet high. These waterfalls also featured colorful names such as Caledonia, Hawthorne, Ribbon, Stairway and Vandevere Cascades.

Caledonia Cascades from a vintage postcard.

A WALK ON THE WILD SIDE - PROFESSOR LEON CHEATS DEATH

The Great Wallenda's legendary 1970 walk across Tallulah Gorge is still well known today, but many do not realize that Wallenda was not the first to risk his life crossing Tallulah on a high wire. In 1886, when Tallulah Falls was still in its wild early years, local hotel owner W. D. Young witnessed a high-wire walk between two buildings at Five Points on Peachtree Street in Atlanta. Young was duly impressed, and as he was always looking to draw crowds to Tallulah Falls, he decided to meet the daring acrobat.

The performer's name was Mr. J. A. St. John, known professionally as Professor Leon. In addition to being a daring aerialist, Leon was notable as the son of the 1884 Prohibition Party presidential candidate. Young spoke with the famed aerialist, enticing him to take his act both higher and farther, and reportedly offered him $250 to attempt the daring feat.

Though similar walks had been accomplished in the 1850s at world-renowned Niagara Falls, the walk across Tallulah Gorge was billed as both the highest and longest high-wire walk ever attempted. Thousands of feet of heavy hemp rope were required for the feat, which included the main cable and dozens of attached guy wires required to keep the main line from swaying. Leon reportedly strung the main cable himself, actually descending to the river, carrying the rope across, then climbing back up to the opposite rim. Professor Leon's daring route would begin near Point Inspiration on the north rim and reach across to Lovers' Leap on the south rim. The height of the main rope that Leon was to cross was at the time estimated to be around 1,000 feet above the rushing waters of the gorge floor.

On July 24, 1886, the day for the daunting walk dawned. Over one dozen excursion trains pulling nearly 100 passenger coaches entered remote Tallulah Falls, reportedly coming from as far away as South Carolina, Florida and Alabama. A massive crowd estimated at upwards of 6,000 people descended upon the tiny town to witness this death-defying walk. Vendors offered beer to the gathering crowd, while Mr. Young sold photographs of Professor Leon. Interest in the daunting walk was unusually keen among betters, and odds were set anywhere from even to 2-to-1 that Professor Leon would not complete the walk.

19th century publicity shot of Professor Leon

At approximately 5:20 p.m., the Professor stepped onto the line near Inspiration Point and began his dizzying jaunt south. He carried a 46 lb., 30-ft. long pole to help maintain his balance. Just over 1,000 feet away, Professor Leon's wife and four-year-old daughter anxiously waited on the south rim. A local newspaper reported that the spectators, who lined every available nook along the rim and filled the porches of the surrounding hotels, had looks of anxiety and fear on their faces.

Leon began the walk rather methodically, and was more than one-quarter of the way across when a loud snapping noise pierced the air. One of the principal guy lines had given way, and spectators were stunned as the main line holding the professor began to sway several feet! After several terrifying moments in which Leon exercised a series of exaggerated movements to remain balanced, he took several steps forward, dropped to one knee, then calmly sat on the rope.

One of Professor Leon's assistants raced to repair the dangling line. A frightening cry rose from the gorge as word spread that the line had been deliberately cut. Though tensions remained high, Leon waited as the damaged guy line was retied. Lookouts were posted to protect the remaining lines.

After approximately nine minutes, the Professor returned to his feet and completed the crossing. Several witnesses claim that Leon was livid, even talking to himself when he finally reached the safety of the south rim. The entire event had taken only about twenty-five minutes. Leon's wife was said to have fainted as soon as the crossing was completed.

The exhausted Professor and his family were immediately escorted to the nearby Grand View Hotel to recover from the stress and strain of the unusually dramatic events. Though the Professor's contract called for a return trip across the gorge, Young decided that, under the unusual circumstances, Leon had more than fulfilled his part of the agreement. Additionally, Leon's personal physician and members of the assembled crowd also begged him not to risk his life again.

The mystery surrounding the cut guy line was never solved. It is theorized that someone wagering against the Professor cut the line in order to collect on a bet. Professor Leon survived both gorge and man that day, and wisely disappeared from Tallulah Falls. Though local folks aren't sure, some say he lost his life some years later attempting to cross Niagara Falls.

THE FASCINATING LIFE OF TALLULAH FALLS' COLORFUL COUNT

One of the most fascinating personalities in the early years of the town was not only a man of many talents, but of several names as well. The man was Dr. Percy Trant Hickson Norcop. Dr. Norcop, whose family name was originally Norcock, lived from 1853 to 1922, and was also known as Dr. Duboeay, or Count Duboeay. He was educated at the Royal College of Physicians and Royal College of Surgeons in Edinburgh and received the distinction of being named a fellow of both prestigious institutions.

One of his professors at Edinburgh was Sir Joseph Lister. Another professor, Dr. Charles Watson Mac-Gillvary, described his former student in a letter of introduction meant for Dr. Norcop's entrance into American society, as "being one of the best educated young medical men of my acquaintance, well read, not only in purely medical subjects, but also possessed of a vast fund of general and scientific information." And, as the Norcock family had done for generations, Percy served in the British Royal Navy.

Dr. Percy Trant Hickson Norcop and his wife, the former Sarah Leicester Hunnicutt.

When Percy was thirty years old, Count Edouard

St. Algier de Duboeay of St. Malo, France, offered to make the much younger Norcop his legal heir if he would change his name to Duboeay. The physician obliged the ailing aristocrat, filing the legal name change in England's Chancery Division of the High Court of Justice in 1883, becoming Percy Trant St. Algier de Duboeay. But even this name change did not last long, as an addendum to the legal document was filed about a month later, stating, "At the request of my mother, Margaret G. Norcop, I will use the surname of Norcop as a second Christian name and instead of the name Trant - Signing as Percy Norcop St. A. de Duboeay."

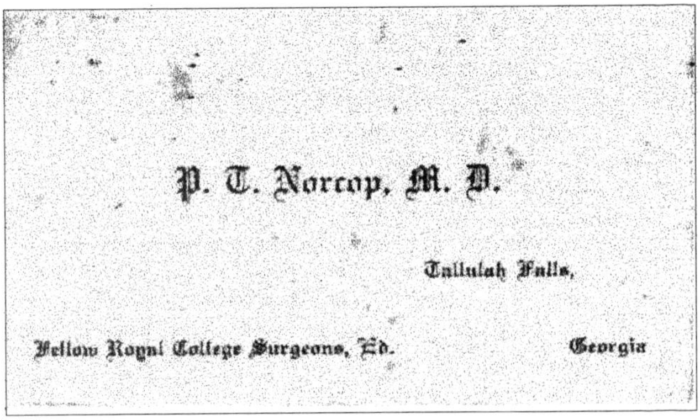

A copy of the good doctor's Tallulah Falls business card states "Fellow Royal College Surgeons, Ed."

The now Dr. Duboeay returned to America, where he and his mother, Margaret Georgina Hickson Norcop (1820-1894), had been residing in Asheville, North Carolina. It was in North Carolina that Percy met and married a beautiful heiress by the name of Minnie Leigh Tunis. Embarking on a European honeymoon in July, 1882, the couple went to Ireland to meet members of Percy's family, including his cousin Sir Maurice Fitzgerald, and was entertained at the various family estates in County Kerry, where Percy's mother was born. But the marriage was shortlived, as the young Mrs. Norcop left her husband while still honeymooning and filed for divorce.

After numerous hearings in both the United States and England, the divorce was granted in June, 1886. Minnie Tunis Norcop remained in

The beautiful Glenbrook Hotel, once the home of Dr. and Mrs. Norcop.. Early 1900s postcard, published by the Artvue Post Card Co., New York.

Europe and within two years married Carroll Mercer of Baltimore at Saint Martin in the Fields, Westminster, London. They later became the parents of Lucy Mercer Rutherford, Franklin Roosevelt's beloved "Missy" who was with the President when he died at the Little White House in Warm Springs, GA (quickly departing before First Lady Eleanor Roosevelt arrived at the scene of her husband's sudden demise).

During the lengthy legailites of obtaining a divorce, Dr. Norcop had met and fallen in love with Sarah Leicester Hunnicutt of Tallulah Falls, who was traveling with her father, William McEwen Hunnicutt. William Hunnicutt, a Confederate veteran and former Clerk of the Superior Court of Rabun County, was in very poor health as a result of being wounded and suffering harsh imprisonment at the hands of the Yankees during the War Between the States. The divorce finally granted, Dr. Norcop married his beloved "Chummie," as he called her, and moved to Tallulah Falls around 1890. Here he built the opulent Glenbrook Chateau as a wedding gift for his bride. The couple later had one child, a daughter, Margaret.

About Tallulah Falls, Dr. Duboeay is said to have remarked, "Such wonderful works of the Omnipotent make men pause in wondrous admiration," while the silence of the region was "broken only by distant cannonading of Tallulah's mighty waterfalls against the river rocks, sounding to the ear as though some great battle was in progress over the hills beyond, and when even and anon sounds of heavy siege guns thundering forth defiance in the grand explosions of artillery." (*Athens Banner,* May 20, 1900.)

The good doctor, who changed his name from Duboeay back to Norcop when he became an American citizen, was considered somewhat of a mystery figure during his time in Tallulah Falls, and as such, much has been said about him which has no basis in fact. Older residents remembered him as a physician held in high esteem in the community. Others have recited numerous exotic rumors about his mysterious exodus from Europe.

One story, denied by many close to the Count, states that he left England in a considerable amount of undisclosed trouble. Yet another story is that Norcop fled France after the fall of Napoleon III. Perhaps the most bizarre story of all is the rumor, circulated for years, that Norcop committed suicide by hanging himself in the non-existent bell tower at Glenbrook after the inn had gone out of business. In reality, Dr. Norcop died quietly at St. Joseph's Hospital in Atlanta on September 14, 1922, the local newspapers extolling his fine attributes as an outstanding physician.

While many of the mysterious details of his tantalizing past remain uncertain, Dr. Duboeay/Norcop seems to have for the most part led a quiet and respectable life in the good town of Tallulah Falls. The Count opened the Red Cross Museum of Historical Relics and Curiosities in Tallulah Falls around 1900. The museum featured interesting items from an extensive collection of artifacts, including a Columbus Bible, Civil War memorabilia, and items from his Napoleon and Marie Antionette collection.

One of the more interesting stories states that Duboeay gave a local hotel owner's wife (Mrs. Robinson of Robinson's Hotel fame) a cup and saucer reportedly hand-painted by Marie Antoinette herself. A member of Dr. Norcop's family recalls seeing a tea service that had belonged to

Marie Antoinette, once displayed in Norcop's museum and later used by the family, featured as a highlight of an antiques and fine arts exhibit in Milledgeville a number of years ago. Another of the museum's treasures was a portrait of Pauline Bonaparte by the French Master Jacques-Louis David. But, alas, the hard times of the Great Depression necessitated the sale of the painting to a private collector.

When Norcop's mother died in 1894, she was interred in the small family chapel on the grounds of Glenbrook. As one of the first Roman Catholics in the area, Dr. Norcop had the chapel constructed for private family worship. It later became the first Catholic house of worship in Rabun County. Monsignor Francis Xavier Bazin from Augusta would visit and celebrate Mass in the chapel.

After the family sold Glenbrook, the chapel was demolished and the remains of Margaret Hickson Norcop were relocated to the Rock Mountain Cemetery on the north side of Tallulah Gorge. Twenty-eight years later, Dr. Norcop joined his mother as he was laid to rest in his adopted hometown of Tallulah Falls. The wall that originally surrounded the Norcop family plot no longer exists, and a family descendant has replaced the older grave markers with newer ones that list reportedly innaccurate dates.

Author's note: J.V. Michael Motes of Marietta, GA, provided photographs and much of the factual material on Dr. Norcop. He is a great-great nephew of Dr. and Mrs. Norcop, and has a large collection of personal papers and photographs pertaining to the family which he eventually plans to publish.

SHADES OF LOCH NESS! THE GREAT BEAST OF TALLULAH GORGE

In 1891, five years after Professor Leon's daring walk brought thousands to Tallulah Falls, an amazing story appeared in the May 17 edition of the *Athens-Banner*. The headline read "A Sensational Finding of a Hideous Monster - in the Tallulah River."

Reportedly, a mysterious creature had been washed ashore at a pool known as Hinkle's Hole by unusually high waters from recent rainstorms. This beast had been pinned against a tree, apparently injured, and had a snakelike body which measured nearly forty-feet long! After the initial hysteria subsided, the beast was remeasured, and the official measurement was reduced to a mere twenty-seven feet.

This strange beast possessed the head of an alligator, a torso similar to a rattlesnake, and a series of short legs or paddles along its body. It had remained hidden in the cold, dark pools of Tallulah Gorge for decades, perhaps even centuries, though a summer resident claimed, after the fact, to have glimpsed the beast on several occasions.

A person who approached the monster with a large pole had it snatched by the beast and broken into pieces. A number of locals tried to destroy the horrible creature, but rifle balls reportedly bounced off its unnaturally tough head before being killed by a shot through the eye.

After it was safely dead, the beast was cut open, and according to the newspaper article, discovered inside were "a number 8 pair of boots, a nice suit of clothes, coat and vest, about half worn in, a waterbury watch, a bottle of whiskey and a deck of cards, one set of brass cuff bottoms with the initials 'T.D.' Some of the boys said it was a town dude the monster had swallowed." There was also mention of a sign which read "Grand View Hotel" found in the beast's belly.

The last mention of the hideous monster was that it had been skinned, and its hide was being displayed first at the Grand View Hotel, then on to the Columbian World's Exposition. Unfortunately, or perhaps conveniently, the hide cannot be found to this day, and no photographs of this strange monster have survived into modern times.

"AUNT" FANNIE PICKLESIMER SMITH - SINKING MOUNTAIN'S LEGENDARY HOSTESS

Nineteenth century Tallulah Falls was renowned for its unmatched natural beauty. Visitors who had been lured into the area by the spectacular scenery soon grew accustomed to the graceful southern hospitality of the town's inns and boarding houses, which included sumptuous dining. Ironically, the area's greatest hostess didn't even live in Tallulah Falls, but rather seven hard miles away in a simple log cabin located at the foot of an enigmatic landmark known locally as Sinking Mountain.

Known affectionately to everyone as "Aunt" Fannie, Fannie Picklesimer was born just across the North Carolina line on March 9, 1825 to Abraham and Eleanor Hooper Picklesimer. Like many young ladies of her day, Fannie married quite early. At the tender age of sixteen, Fannie became the wife of William Rufus Kerby, who shortly thereafter set about building the family home at the isolated southeast Rabun County landmark Sinking Mountain.

Unfortunately, Fannie was widowed in 1849, after just eight years of marriage. She now found herself alone with four small children in the harsh southern Appalachian backwoods. In 1852, twenty-seven year old Fannie remarried, this time to Ambrose J. Smith. Aunt Fannie's family was complete once more, and the couple continued to live in the cabin below Sinking Mountain.

Fannie Smith's family continued to grow, and she eventually bore eleven children, including ten daughters! Her only son, Wilson Hamilton Kerby, served for a while in the Confederate Army. Fannie's first husband, William Kerby, had selected a good parcel of land, for it quickly

Aunt Fannie sits in her mule-drawn wagon, preparing to head back to the cabin after enduring the rugged seven-mile ride into Tallulah Falls.

became known as one of the most productive farms in the area. According to some of Aunt Fannie's descendants, Cherokee Indians actually camped on the Smith property in the cold winter months in order to partake of the abundance of food produced on the farm.

As Tallulah Falls began its rapid growth in the 1870s, the reputation of the frail, dark-eyed Aunt Fannie began to grow as well. Accustomed to feeding a large family, Aunt Fannie began to offer meals to visitors in the area. Literally thousands endured the bumpy seven-mile journey to feast on Aunt Fannie's famous fried chicken, some staying for days or even weeks with the famous hostess. For over twenty-five years, this industrious mountain woman ran one of the most profitable businesses in the area. Guests from near and far, both the ordinary and famous, made the trek to Sinking Mountain to sample Aunt Fannie's unmatched fare.

Besides her role as a world-class hostess, Aunt Fannie was also quite active in both her church and in local politics. As her own daughters grew and eventually left home, she is said to have personally selected and trained numerous local girls to assist in the family business. Aunt Fannie remained healthy and active well into her eighties. The legendary hostess of Sinking Mountain passed away on May 20, 1914, never realizing the extent to which her fame had spread.

Aunt Fannie hard at work at her spinning wheel on the open porch of her rustic home near Tallulah Falls.

Much of the background information on Aunt Fannie came from Michael Motes' excellent aricle - "Aunt Fannie Smith - the Famous Hostess of Sinking Mountain," Georgia Magazine, *August 1971. Anyone interested in more information about Aunt Fannie should obtain a copy of this article.*

WALTER HUNNICUTT (INC.)
PHOTOGRAPHER, PUBLISHER, ENTREPRENEUR

Many of the outstanding photographs capturing the early history of Tallulah Falls were made by one extraordinary man - Walter Hunnicutt. Born in 1860, Hunnicutt became interested in the fledgling art of photography early on. From the grand hotel era in the 1880s through the depression-era decade of the 1930s, Hunnicutt captured thousands of images of people and places in and around Tallulah Falls using a heavy large format wooden dry-plate camera. Hunnicutt's photo studio in Tallulah Falls was a town fixture during the town's bustling early years.

Like many other mountain residents of yesteryear, Hunnicutt was a multi-talented man. He developed an ability for creating twig furniture, most notably from the abundant stands of mountain laurel found in the area. Hunnicutt put this ability to good use, opening the Rustic Furniture Company. His creations graced many of the homes and hotels in Tallulah Falls. In a completely unrelated career, Hunnicutt operated the Tallulah Drug Company for a number of years.

A Blue Ridge Mountain Postcard Co. postcard showing the Cliff House Hotel.

One of Hunnicutt's more interesting ventures was into publishing. As Tallulah Falls was a popular tourist destination drawing thousands of visitors each year, Hunnicutt began producing a series of postcards. These cards were published either under his name, or under Blue Ridge Mountain Post Card Company.

Hunnicutt is also well known for his venture into the newspaper business as publisher of Rabun County's first newspaper, the appropriately named *Tallulah Falls Spray* (subscription in 1897 - one dollar per year).

Truly a man of great energy and talent, Hunnicutt reportedly worked around town as a painter on occasion.

Though he died in 1931, Hunnicutt's photographic legacy provides us today with perhaps the greatest visual evidence of Tallulah Falls' rich history.

Walter Thomas Hunnicutt

DEVILS PULPIT, 750 FEET HIGH, TALLULAH FALLS, GA.
Copyright Feb. 1st, 1907, by Walter Hunnicutt.

Devil's Pulpit postcard, published in 1907 by Walter Hunnicutt.

"ANYBODY SEEN MY BULLDOZER?" MYSTERIOUS SINKING MOUNTAIN

Even though the primary draw in Tallulah Falls was the unmatched natural beauty of the gorge and falls, there were a few local curiosities which drew visitors as well. One of these, mysterious Sinking Mountain, was located about four miles north of the gorge (as the crow flies), and only a short walk from famed Aunt Fannie's cabin.

As seen from the south and west, Sinking Mountain was rather unremarkable, rising slightly from the surrounding terrain. However, its eastern flank was quite dramatic, plunging wildly into the foreboding Chattooga River gorge over six hundred feet below. Those who walked to the summit gained a dramatic vantage point for enjoying the surrounding scenery. Early visitors noticed that if they stood in certain spots, the ground seemed remarkably soft, almost giving way underfoot. As with any other interesting landmark of its day, a legend was soon born.

Early settlers and visitors began to accept the Cherokee explanation for the occurence, which was that Tallulah Gorge's infamous "little people," the Yunwi Tsundi, were responsible for this strange phenomenon. The story goes that the little people were involved in a large mining operation within the mountain, and that this was the cause of the sinking effect. Visitors to the area today will swear that the ground does have a strange feel to it, and witnesses today claim that heavy earthmoving equipment left parked here for several days have been known to sink as much as two feet. An August 5, 1885 article in the Athens *Banner-Watchman* related that it did not greatly impress everyone:

> The mountain continues to go down. We spent last Sunday with Mrs. Smith, who lives at its base, but owing to the wet weather did not make the ascent. It is not much of an attraction, and we had much rather view the scenery from the summit of Rock Mountain, only three miles from the hotel. It is a long and very rough ride to the Sinking Mountain.

LOUIS B. MAGID and the GREAT TALLULAH FALLS SILK ENTERPRISE

Around the turn of the twentieth century Tallulah Falls proved to be a magnet for entrepreneurs of all types. Many came here to make their fortunes building hotels, developing land, constructing the railroad, or tapping the Tallulah's vast hydroelectric potential. One man, Louis B. Magid, seemed to have a hand in nearly all of these, including one fascinating venture that was a dream of Georgia founder James Ogelthorpe in the early 1700s - silk.

Louis Boris Magid was born in Germany in 1874, and at one time or another worked as an engineer, banker, financier, publisher, realtor and silk merchant. Magid was drawn to the Tallulah Falls area as a railroad financier, working with then Tallulah Falls Railway president George Prentiss to raise capital for the proposed extension northward to Franklin, North Carolina. After witnessing the Tallulah River's awesome power around 1901, he began buying land around the gorge, reportedly for their valuable water power options.

About the same time, Magid formed the Magid-Hope Silk Company in Boston, MA., and journeyed to Europe attempting to raise money for his silk ventures. Looking for a suitable location to begin a silk farming operation in the United States, Magid was evidently intrigued by the possibilities offered by the Tallulah Falls area. With the support of Prentiss, Magid began developing a mulberry plantation adjacent to the railroad line in nearby Tallulah Park. In September, 1902, Magid's Seri-Culture and Manufacturing Company filed charter in Atlanta, with Magid as the president and George Prentiss as one of his directors.

Magid's immediate goal with Seri-Culture was to build silk mills for the reeling and manufacturing of raw silk and silk yarns. Long range plans included a silk plantation encompassing over 3,500 acres to be run primarily by Italian immigrants with a strong background in silk production. A prospectus of the planned enterprise called for the development of a town along the railroad line that included a silk and industrial college, granary for silkworms and eggs, a lake and powerhouse.

In 1903, Magid began experimenting with production of colored silk and fishing lines. In December of that same year he began publishing *Silk* magazine, a publication dedicated to promoting the silk industry. By 1905, Magid claimed to have 200,000 mulberry trees growing on the rolling hillsides near Tallulah Lodge. News of Magid's developing enterprise spread across the country, and in 1905 he became president of the Silk Culture League of America. Magid's name had become synonymous with the silk industry in America.

Always the consummate entrepreneur, there has been considerable conjecture that Magid's proposed silk development was closely tied to his dreams of developing the Tallulah Falls area's vast hydroelectric potential. Magid evidently planned to operate his silk plants with electricity produced at his own hydroelectric developments, then sell the excess power to developing towns and industries located along the Tallulah Falls Railroad line.

Unfortunately for those who dreamed of vast fortunes in silk, Magid's lofty expectations never materialized. The exact reasons remain somewhat of a mystery to this day, but it is thought that Magid may have overestimated the economic benefits of producing silk, or perhaps he found the Tallulah Falls climate not as suitable as first expected. It seemed that Magid had so many other business ideas and ventures that he walked away from the Tallulah Falls silk project.

Magid's main business interest in the Tallulah Falls area thereafter involved developing lots for second homes through his Tallulah Park Land Company. Years later Magid was known to have been involved in an apple orchard operation, sold automobiles, and founded the Louis B. Magid Investment Bankers organization. Though his ambitious plans for the area never materialized, Louis Magid's name is forever a part of the colorful history of Tallulah Falls.

"SAY CHEESE, PLEASE"
WATCHING THE BIRDIE AT TALLULAH FALLS

Photographers such as the versatile Walter Hunnicutt were primarily responsible for much of the splendid images we have of Tallulah Falls in the colorful days of the late 1800s. Unfortunately, photographers of that era did not have polaroids, instamatics or digital cameras. In the nineteenth century, "point and shoot" was what you did while hunting, or if you found your wife with another man. The photographic equipment of Tallulah Falls' early days was often large and cumbersome, and required great effort to transport into the gorge.

However, one similarity to the late eighteenth century remains. Just as in modern times, early visitors loved to have their photographs taken in the wild setting of Tallulah. Whether it be posing at a lofty overlook or next to a rugged rock formation in the heart of the gorge, hundreds of photographs from the wild early days remind modern day explorers that Tallulah's magic extends well back into recent history.

Vintage postcard shows a small group of visitors hamming it up during their visit to the gorge.

Above: A rather well-dressed group of proper ladies pose along the river in the gorge. Courtesy of the Georgia Department of Archives and History.

Below: A mixed group of bathers and would-be bathers pose on the back side of Tallulah Lake near the lower end of River Street circa 1920s.

Notice any similarities? Each photograph on this page was made at the same location in Tallulah Gorge. Below: A group of sightseers circa 1900. Note the gentleman on the right holding the camera. Several people in these photos seem to be carrying hiking sticks - still a good idea today. Bottom photo courtesy of the Georgia Department of Archives and History.

BUILDING THE DAMS THAT HARNASSED THE MIGHTY TALLULAH

In the late 1800s and early 1900s North Georgia was a land of great opportunity for those seeking to tap into its great wealth of natural resources. Early industrialists saw great potential in the mineral deposits and timber of the region. Others familiar with the vast economic potential of electricity had their eyes on other resources, and the powerful waters of the Tallulah River were the primary focus of their attention. The city of Atlanta, ninety miles to the south, was developing an enormous appetite for this modern resource, and Tallulah Falls was part of the solution.

Though a number of individuals or companies were interested in developing Tallulah Falls into a hydroelectric plant, it was the Georgia

The Tallulah Falls dam nears completion in 1913.
Photo courtesy of the Georgia Power Corporate Archives.

Railway and Power Company that actually accomplished this incredible engineering feat. The Georgia Railway and Power Company was born in 1912 from the merger of the Georgia Railway and Electric Company and the Georgia Power Company. The Georgia Railway and Electric Company had previously been formed in 1902 by Henry M. Atkinson. The Georgia Power Company was organized in 1908 by C. Elmer Smith and Eugene Ashley. Though none of these men were originally from the South, they each realized the incredible potential of electrical generation and distribution, and saw the potential of the Tallulah's waters.

Construction of these dams took place from 1911 to 1927. The first to be built was the Tallulah Falls dam, a massive 126-foot tall gravity arch concrete structure stretching 426-feet across the upper gorge adjacent to the town of Tallulah Falls. The mammoth dam would form 63-acre Tallulah Lake, and a huge underground tunnel would transport its precious water toward a powerhouse deep within the gorge. The tunnel itself was a tremendous undertaking. Nearly 20 men labored furiously for 15 months to build the 6,666-foot tunnel approximately 100 feet below ground. The tunnel emerged

Workers deep within the underground water tunnel. Courtesy of the Georgia Power Corporate Archives.

from underground high above the powerhouse, where six huge penstocks allowed the water to accelerate into the gorge and powerplant. A breathtaking incline railway system capable of carrying men and equipment ran to the construction site at the bottom of the gorge.

Six huge penstocks transport the water from the underground diversion tunnel into the Tallulah Falls powerhouse. Photo courtesy of the Georgia Power Corporate Archives.

During this time, thousands of workers descended into the Tallulah basin to work on the project. Over 46 miles of the Tallulah River would be affected by the construction, with a total drop of nearly 1,200 vertical feet from the backwaters of Lake Burton to Yonah dam on the Tugalo River below Tallulah Falls. Since the area was largely inaccessible, spur lines were constructed from the Tallulah Falls Railroad mainline out to each dam site, making possible the transportation of men, machinery and materials necessary for a massive construction project of this type.

The Tallulah Falls hydroelectric project was considered one the great engineering feats of its day. At the time of its construction (1912-1913), the dam was one of the highest in the eastern U.S., and the electrical output of 60,000 kilowatts (expanded to 72,000 kw in 1919) was also among the greatest at that time. Five other dams were eventually com-

A massive piece of equipment heads down the incline railroad toward the powerhouse in the bottom of the gorge. Photo courtesy of the Georgia Power Corporate Archives.

pleted; Terrora dam (1915) forming 834-acre Lake Rabun; Tugalo dam (1923) forming 597-acre Lake Tugalo; Yonah dam (1925) forming 325-acre Lake Yonah; Nacoochee dam (1926) forming 240-acre Lake Seed; Burton dam (1927) forming 2,775-acre Lake Burton.

The total electrical generating capacity for the entire series of six dams eventually reached over 166,000 kilowatts.

A group of engineers working on the hydro project pose for a photograph circa 1913.

Many today take the beautiful string of mountain lakes created by these great dams for granted. Several generations have passed since the early 1900s when thousands of men labored nearly fifteen years to build these impressive structures. Though some may bemoan the loss of a wild and free Tallulah River, there can be no doubt that the massive construction project brought jobs, development, and electricity into the once remote area. The pioneering era of dam construction altered the face of Tallulah Falls and Tallulah Gorge forever.

The completed Tallulah dam in 1914. This dam was an "intake" dam; it served to impound water for the purpose of diverting it into the underground penstocks for its journey to the powerhouse. Note the structures on the far bank of the lake just behind the dam. These house a series of gates leading to two underground tunnels. For over twenty-five years the top of the dam served as the motor vehicle route across the gorge. Photo courtesy of the Georgia Power Corporate Archives.

"YOU'LL BE HEARING FROM MY LAWYER" THE GREAT LEGAL BATTLE FOR THE FALLS

Around the turn of the century while Tallulah Falls was still enjoying unprecedented popularity among sightseers and tourists, industrialists began eying this untapped natural resource as a source for hydroelectric power generation. Power interests practically drooled over Tallulah Gorge with its abundant water and six hundred foot elevation drop. But the gorge was merely the centerpiece of a much larger network of proposed dams and lakes in the region.

One of America's first great conservation battles was fought here in the early 1900s over the proposed dams on the Tallulah River. This battle was led by Helen Dortch Longstreet, widow of Confederate commander General James Longstreet. In 1911, Mrs. Longstreet organized the *Tallulah Falls Conservation Association* into a statewide effort aimed at raising funds to fight the acquisition of the falls by various power company interests. Mrs. Longstreet's primary goal was to see Tallulah Gorge become a state park, and thus be preserved in its natural state in perpetuity. Though several individuals and companies had been acquiring land along the rim of the gorge for a number of years, Mrs. Longstreet's fight centered on the argument that early surveys indicated that all points below the rim of the gorge, including the Tallulah River, belonged to the state.

The fight to save the falls raged even after the Georgia Railway and Power Company became legal owner of the lands in dispute along the gorge rim. Construction on Tallulah dam at the head of the gorge was well underway by the time the case went to court. The case first came to trial in Rabun County Superior Court in the spring of 1913, with the state of Georgia filing suit against the power company. After losing the first verdict, the state appealed the case to the state Supreme Court. When the final verdict came in, the court concluded that the property within Tallulah Gorge did indeed belong to the Georgia Railway and Power Company. Work on the dam continued, and was soon completed.

In September, 1913, the first electricity produced from Tallulah's powerful waters began flowing over newly constructed lines to the booming state capital of Atlanta, ninety miles to the south. The fight to keep the Tallulah flowing wild and free was finally over, and the landscape of Tallulah Falls was forever altered. The songful falls were now muted, and with paved highways reaching further into the developing Blue Ridge, Tallulah Falls now had another battle on the horizon - the fight to keep visitors coming to the gorge.

Two sightseeing couples enjoy the magnificent view as they gaze upstream toward Young's bridge before construction of the dam. Note the distant train crossing the trestle over the town of Tallulah Falls. Construction of Tallulah dam would take place in the general area shown at the base of this photograph, drastically altering this scene.

THE GENERAL'S WIFE LEADS THE CHARGE TO KEEP THE FALLS FREE

Great conservation battles seem destined to be identified with one person, such as John Muir's efforts to preserve beautiful Yosemite. The fight to save Tallulah Falls from developers was no different, and the individual who organized and led much of the campaign to save the falls was Mrs. Helen Dortch Longstreet.

Born in 1863, Mrs. Longstreet hailed from nearby Carnesville, approximately thirty miles south of Tallulah Falls. At the time she entered the Tallulah Falls fray around 1905, Mrs. Longstreet was already well known in the state as the widow of distinguished Confederate General James Longstreet. Interestingly, Mrs. Longstreet and the general did not marry until 1897, thirty-two years after the conclusion of the Civil War. At the time they married, Mrs. Longstreet was thirty-four and the General a spry seventy-six.

After their marriage, the couple lived peacefully in Gainesville, where Mrs. Longstreet had attended Brenau College. There General Longstreet ran a local hotel and served as postmaster. After his death in 1904, Mrs. Longstreet was appointed Georgia's first postmistress.

Mrs. Longstreet did not become fully involved in the battle for Tallulah Falls until around 1911, when work on the dam at Tallulah Falls was well underway. Mrs. Longstreet organized the *Tallulah Falls Conservation Association* to lead the fight. Though primarily an organization for women, Mrs. Longstreet labored hard to raise money, awareness and participants for her cause, even pledging her $2,600 salary as postmistress, and incurring a personal $5,000 debt to fund the battle.

Mrs. Longstreet, never one to be accused of timidity, took her fight right to the top. During the years the issue was in question, she met with the state attorney general, Georgia Governor Hoke Smith, contacted President Taft, and initiated a legal battle with the powerful Georgia Railway and Power Company.

When Mrs. Longstreet proved unable to persuade the governor or attorney general to bring suit on behalf of the state, she began an intensive and often bitter lobbying campaign for passage of a resolution in the state legislature. The resolution stated that since the land in question within Tallulah Gorge had never been surveyed, the interests of the state should be ascertained and protected. When Mrs. Longstreet's resolution finally made it out of committee and the full House voted on it, her resolution was approved by a vote of 112 to 19. Mrs. Longstreet's efforts had finally forced the issue into the Georgia courts.

Though both the initial court verdict and the appeal came in on the side of the power interests, Mrs. Longstreet had fought the good fight. She lived an additional fifty years beyond the great Tallulah Falls preservation battle, passing away in 1962 at the grand old age of 99. A portion of those years were spent defending the efforts of her dearly departed husband, the General, from detractors who blamed him for the Confederate loss at the battle of Gettysburg.

Some who knew her claim that she eventually grew to love the beautiful manmade chain of lakes she so bitterly opposed. Though she did not live long enough to see her beloved Tallulah Gorge become the park she so coveted, she certainly would have been surprised at how the park came about some thirty years after her death; namely, through the combined efforts of the initial adversaries in the battle - the state of Georgia and Georgia Power Company.

Secrets of Tallulah
AFTER THE DAMS
1914 - Present

TALLULAH FALLS SCHOOL SHINES A WELCOME LIGHT IN THE MOUNTAINS

In the early 1900s most mountain children in the Tallulah Falls area suffered from a severe lack of educational opportunities. The rural mountain economy still had not developed to the point where every child could attend school. Mrs. Mary Ann Lipscomb, a prominent summer resident from Athens, was so moved by the plight of these children that she led a movement through the Georgia Federation of Women's Clubs to establish the Tallulah Falls Industrial School, which first opened its doors in 1909.

The school grew rapidly from its inception, and for some time served as the public school for the Tallulah Falls area. Students attending the school received not only an academic education, but instruction in various industrial work as well. As Rabun and Habersham counties began developing their own public school systems in the 1950s, enrollment at Tallulah Falls School began to diminish. The school met this challenge

1909 photo from the school's first year shows teacher Miss Annie Thrasher and her attentive students. Photo courtesy of Tallulah Falls School Museum.

Early Tallulah Falls School students and their "transportation" pose in front of what appears to be the long railroad trestle adjacent to River Street. Photo courtesy of Tallulah Falls School Musuem.

by expanding its outreach from local to regional. In 1970, Tallulah Falls School assumed its present form as a private boarding school.

As it nears its first century mark, Tallulah Falls School has grown from its initial enrollment of twenty-one local students and one teacher to nearly one hundred-fifty students and a broad staff of approximately seventy-five highly talented educators. The facilities have been steadily improved and expanded as well. Today, Tallulah Falls School continues its mission of being "the light in the mountains," entering a new century and new millennium with an ever-widening mission of excellence in education.

Above: A group of students gather for a photograph in 1922. Photo courtesy of Tallulah Falls School Museum.

Below: A large crowd poses in front of a newly completed school building. This postcard was produced by Walter Hunnicutt's Blue Ridge Post Card Co.

ACCIDENT OR ARSON? THE TOWN BURNS IN THE GREAT FIRE OF 1921

After the completion of Tallulah Falls intake dam in 1913, the legendary falls deep within Tallulah Gorge were reduced to a mere trickle. The gorge remained a place of great natural beauty, but its very soul had been diminished with the diversion of the great river into twin underground tunnels. Curious onlookers still visited Tallulah Falls to witness the massive hydroelectric structures, but most tourists seemed content to catch a brief glimpse of the unnaturally silent gorge from one of the lookout points along the rim as they headed for points higher and further into the developing mountain region. The once-robust tourist town of Tallulah Falls began to languish.

The struggling town suffered another devastating blow in December, 1921, as a destructive fire erupted in an automotive repair shop in the main portion of town. A strong winter wind quickly whipped the blaze into an inferno, with sparks and hot cinders blowing wildly from house-top to housetop. With no city-wide water system or fire department, the

The lower end of Tallulah Falls along River Street before the fire. Note the top of the dam (lower left foreground), and the trestle above the rooftops.

The lower end of town after the fire. Note the remains of the railroad trestle in the background. Photo courtesy Georgia Power Corporate Archives.

townspeople had little chance of fighting the rapidly spreading fire. By the time it had burned itself out, the blaze had consumed hotels, businesses, residences and most of the massive railroad trestle which spanned the rooftops over much of the town.

Though many of the details remain in question, some locals believed that a disgruntled visitor, angry at not receiving immediate help for an automobile stuck in the mud, started the fire in the garage. Wherever the fire actually started, and for whatever reason, the old hotels and other wooden structures destroyed by the fire were gone for good.

The railroad trestle was quickly rebuilt and the old TF resumed service, but most of the town's residents did not carry insurance, and therefore could not afford to rebuild. The town which had struggled for eight long years with decreasing tourism was now dealt yet another crippling blow. In what must be remembered as one of Tallulah Falls' darkest days, decades of grand history were reduced to ashes in a single night, changing the face and character of the town forever.

Those wishing to obtain more information should read "Fire at the Falls!," Harry Bartlett, North Georgia Journal, *Spring 1993.*

"THE GRASS IS ALWAYS GREENER" BRIDGING THE MIGHTY TALLULAH

Tallulah Gorge once presented a formidable natural barrier to those wishing to enter Rabun County from the south. In the resort days, long before Tallulah dam was constructed, several primitive bridges spanned the river upstream of the gorge. The first major structure was built by hotel entrepreneur W. D. Young in 1879. Known (not surprisingly) as Young's Bridge, this iron truss structure was constructed below River Street just above Indian Arrow Rapids, connecting with the old Clayton Road on the north side of the gorge.

The next major advancement in transportation occurred 34 years later with the completion of Tallulah dam. High atop this massive concrete structure a 426-foot single lane roadway connected opposite rims of the upper gorge over 100 feet above the rocky riverbed. This route provided the first real "modern roadway" into Rabun County from the south. The dramatic crossing was used by vehicles of all types, but eventually became obsolete due to increasing traffic.

The first true highway bridge was constructed in 1938-1939. This 505-foot long, two-lane structure was an impressive engineering feat, bridging the gorge nearly 150 feet above the riverbed. A series of massive steel girders were suspended between two towering concrete piers

A group poses for a photograph along the banks of the Tallulah River below one of the early steel truss bridges. This type of one lane bridge was common in the late 1800s and early 1900s in northeast Georgia.

Above: Magnificent view of the concrete support piers as they near completion. Note the spoil pile below the piers on the right. Considerable blasting was required to prepare the steep sides of the gorge to properly anchor the massive piers.

Right: Massive steel girders stretch across the gorge, forming the skeleton for the roadbed. These huge girders were transported to the construction site by the Tallulah Falls Railroad.

View from the southern shore of Tallulah Lake looking north over the top of the dam. Giant cranes swing the massive girders out into position as the U.S. Hwy 23/441 bridge begins to take shape.

anchored in the rocky gorge walls to create this imposing structure. On November 7, 1940, this bridge was dedicated to the memory of Mrs. John King Ottley, President of the Board of Trustees of the Tallulah Falls School from 1922-1940. The dedication address was presented by Preston S. Arkwright, President of Georgia Power Company.

As Rabun County and the higher mountains continued to rapidly develop, increasing traffic caused this structure to become obsolete as well. In 1990-1991, the original two-lane structure was expanded to a full five lanes. This was ingeniously accomplished by utilizing the original concrete piers as the main support structure. This new highway bridge carries thousands of automobiles each day, and provides a dramatic overview of Tallulah dam and the upper gorge for those willing to take a short walk across this historic structure.

Top: Construction workers stand precariously atop one of the huge steel girders shortly after it has been lowered into its mount. Note "Virginia Bridge Co." painted across the top of the girder.

Below: The old and the new stand side by side on a snowy North Georgia day. Automobiles complete the narrow crossing over the top of Tallulah dam as the new highway bridge nears completion. Note the section of railing on the left not yet completed.

ROADSIDE RAMBLES
TALLULAH BECOMES A ROADSIDE ATTRACTION

After massive Tallulah dam was completed in 1913, the awesome gorge lost a great deal of its natural charm. Following the destructive fire of 1921, the town fell even further from of the public eye. Tallulah Falls was no longer the coveted resort it was in the late 1800s, but many tourists driving into the Blue Ridge mountains still paused, even if only for a brief moment, to enjoy the magnificent view.

Only the hardiest of visitors ventured down into the grand chasm. Most seemed content to linger and ponder the now-silent gorge. Since scenic U.S. Hwy 23/441 looped along the eastern end of the gorge before crossing at the dam, several businesses took advantage of a steady flow of traffic by offering meals, snacks, crafts and souvenirs along with a full dose of grand scenery.

Classic old roadside stand "The Gorge View" tempted travelers with fruit, honey and, as the name implied, a great view of Tallulah Gorge.

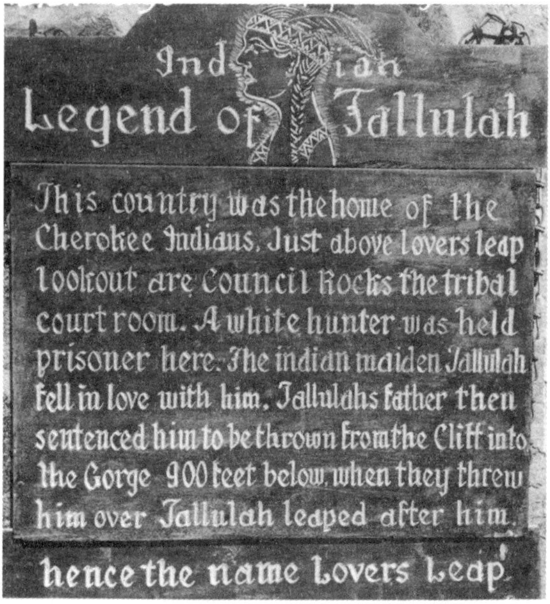
Ind ian
Legend of Tallulah
This country was the home of the
Cherokee Indians. Just above lovers leap
lookout are Council Rocks the tribal
court room. A white hunter was held
prisoner here. The indian maiden Tallulah
fell in love with him. Tallulahs father then
sentenced him to be thrown from the Cliff into
the Gorge 900 feet below. when they threw
him over Tallulah leaped after him.
hence the name Lovers Leap!

Top: Old wooden sign just off the highway relates one version of the story of the Tallulah's famed Lovers' Leap.

Bottom left: Tourist in the 1950s pauses at a Tallulah Gorge historical marker.

Bottom right: Classic old postcard heralds the grand view of dramatic Horseshoe Bend from just off the highway near Tallulah Point.

Three views of famous Harvey's. The top two photos are from the 1930s, and the bottom photo was made in July, 1970, the day Karl Wallenda walked across the gorge. Today, the same building operates as Tallulah Point Overlook, remaining as popular as ever.

Top: Stuckey's operated one of their famous gas station/restaurant businesses for several decades on the northeast corner of the highway bridge. Tallulah Falls School operated a gift shop, museum and nature trail on the same site during the 1980s and early 1990s.

Bottom: A vintage postcard shows the roadside view from Tallulah Point. Hundreds of motorists stop at this site to enjoy the dramatic view of the gorge and surrounding mountains.

THE GREAT WALLENDA STROLLS ACROSS TALLULAH GORGE

On July 18, 1970, eighty-four years after Professor Leon took the first dramatic walk across Tallulah Gorge on a crude hemp rope, legendary aerialist Karl Wallenda came to northeast Georgia to duplicate the amazing feat and revitalize the sagging tourist industry. The walk was staged by Tallulah Productions, a local nonprofit organization attempting to build an amphitheatre in Tallulah Falls.

Wallenda was among the most well-known member of a famous circus family which started in Germany in the 1780s. Karl and his brother,

Publicity still of the Great Wallenda.

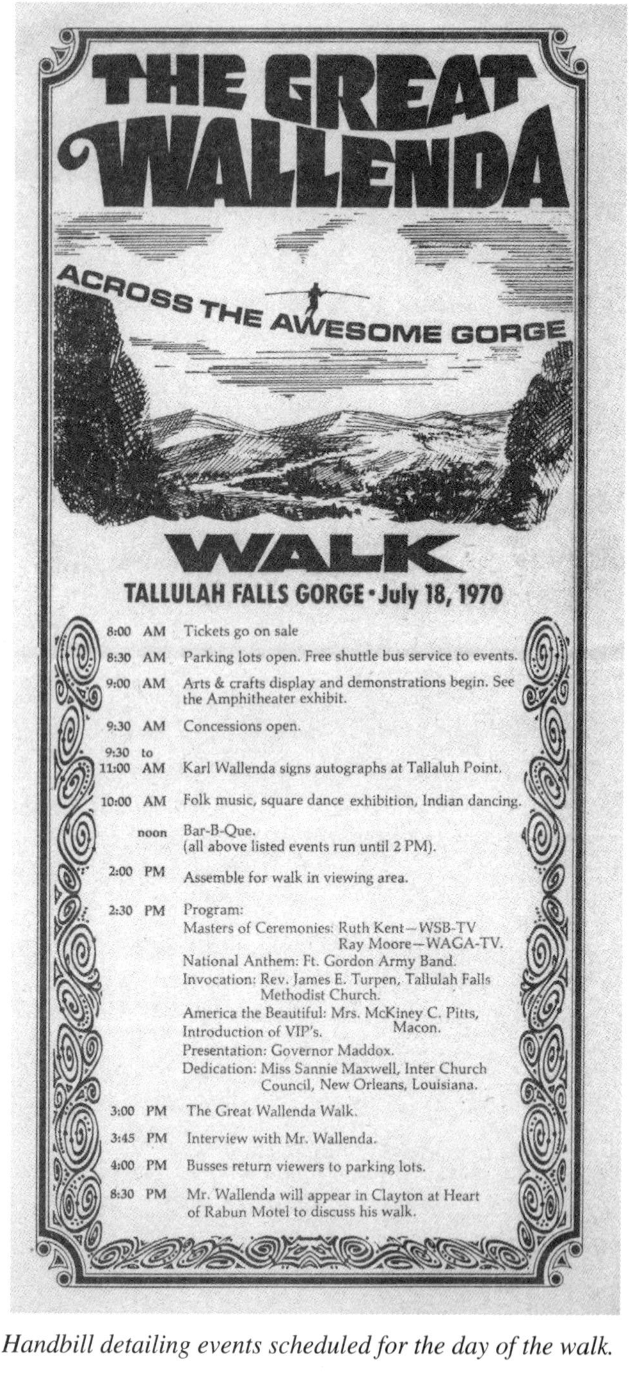

Handbill detailing events scheduled for the day of the walk.

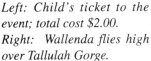

Left: Child's ticket to the event; total cost $2.00.
Right: Wallenda flies high over Tallulah Gorge.

Herman, brought their high-wire act to America in 1928. The family earned legendary status for their aerial feats, but their history was not without its tragedies. During a performance in Detroit in 1962, the Wallendas were performing their signature seven-person pyramid on the high wire. The pyramid collapsed, with each participant falling 40 feet. The accident killed Karl's nephew and son-in-law, and seriously injured his son.

Preparations for Wallenda's walk across Tallulah Gorge began months in advance. The cable was strung between two prefabricated metal towers that had been brought in by helicopter. The north tower reached 30 feet into the air, the south tower about 10 feet. The cable was composed of spun steel, 11/16th of an inch thick, and was stabilized with more than 20,000 additional feet of cable attached at 56 points. Preparing the towers and cable for the walk took a crew of architects, engineers and laborers working 14 hours per day nearly three weeks to complete.

July 18th dawned fair and hot, and a massive crowd estimated at better than 25,000 journied to sleepy Tallulah Falls to witness the show. While Professor Leon's spectators largely came by train, visitors on this day poured into Tallulah Falls by automobile and bus, creating a huge traffic jam. Nearly 700 volunteers were assembled to handle the massive crowd, parking and concession needs. The town took on a carnival atmosphere, as music, square dancing and the enticing smell of barbecue filled the morning air.

Above: A smiling Wallenda casually steadies himself with a heavy balancing pole as he nears the completion of his much publicized walk.

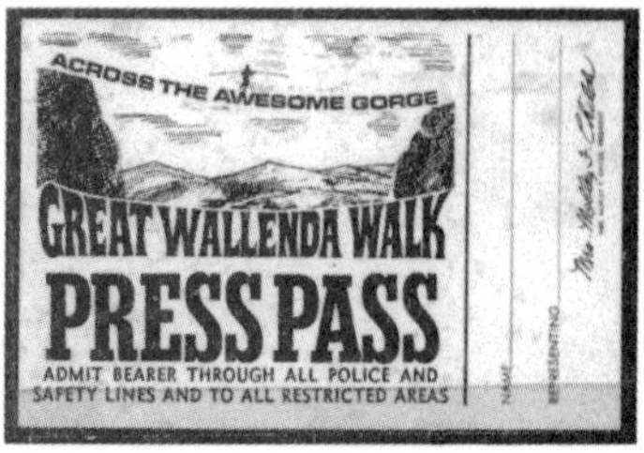

Right: Press credentials for the Great Wallenda walk.

The official festivities began in midafternoon, with several Atlanta television news personalities serving as the masters of ceremonies. The Fort Gordon Army Band played the national anthem, and Reverend James Turpen of Tallulah Falls Methodist Church offered an invocation. After the singing of *America the Beautiful,* and the introduction of VIPs, including Governor Lester Maddox, the walk was set to begin.

Just after three p.m., the 65-year old Wallenda climbed the north rim tower and stepped out onto the cable. The only thing between him and

Professor who? Though some thought Wallenda would keep things simple, he stunned the huge crowd by performing two dramatic headstands.

the opposite rim was 975 feet of steel cable. Wallenda began his trek slowly and methodically, showing no fear or trepidation. Just seconds after leaving the safety of the north rim tower, he found himself nearly 750 feet above the exposed rocks of the rugged gorge floor. As if the walk itself was not dramatic enough, Wallenda paused twice during the trek to perform breathtaking headstands, the second of which he later stated was dedicated to U.S. troops fighting in Vietnam.

The entire walk was completed in about half the time Wallenda had anticipated. As he reached the south rim, The Great Wallenda had covered the distance in slightly less than 18 minutes, requiring 541 well-placed steps. The British Broadcasting Company filmed the walk as part of a documentary on the Great Wallendas. During the walk Wallenda wore a small microphone in order to capture his dramatically unique perspective on the high wire. One of Wallenda's statements while on the wire expressed concern over looking down; another expressed an understandable desire for a martini upon completion of the walk.

The exhausted high wire artist received $10,000 for the afternoon's efforts. Tourists continued to flock to Tallulah Falls in the days and weeks after the walk to see the cable setup and to view the famous scene for themselves. For this reason, the setup was left in place far beyond when it was scheduled to be dismantled. Even today, over 30 years after the daring walk, the rusting remains of the dilapidated towers can still be found on both rims, silent sentinels from the day the Great Wallenda brought the crowds back to Tallulah Falls.

Almost time to celebrate: An obviously relieved Wallenda takes the last careful steps of his walk as he heads uphill toward the safety of the south rim.

HOLLYWOOD RESURRECTS THE MIGHTY TALLULAH FOR "DELIVERANCE"

Though it took several months, life in Tallulah Falls in the post-Wallenda era eventually returned to normal. Things didn't stay quiet for too long, though. In 1972, James Dickey's harrowing novel *Deliverance* was made into a major motion picture. Produced by Warner Bros. and starring Hollywood heavyweights Burt Reynolds, Jon Voight, Ned Beatty and Ronnie Cox, *Deliverance* was filmed primarily on the rugged whitewater of the Chattooga River. The nearby Chauga River in South Carolina and the Tallulah River within the gorge also managed to grab a share of the spotlight.

Through the magic of Hollywood, these three neighboring southern Appalachian streams were cinematically merged to create the fictional Cahulawassee River. The rest, as they say, is movie history. Even though it's been more than three decades since the film's release, the riveting plot, beautiful photography and remarkable musical score have stood the test of time. Though many locals in Rabun County resented the often backwards (and in a few cases, perverted) stereotypes of mountain folks portrayed in the film, *Deliverance* brought fame and notoriety to the area, particularly the Chattooga River.

In one of the film's most dramatic sequences, the principal characters are thrown from their canoes, swept through a series of dramatic rapids and are carried over a thundering waterfall into a huge, still pool. After regrouping on the rocks beneath a towering cliff, "Ed Gentry," played by Jon Voight, attempts a dramatic free climb up the massive, sheer cliff bordering the pool.

These exciting scenes were filmed in the rugged western end of Tallulah Gorge. Since the scene required the river to be flowing at full force, the production company had to secure the help of Georgia Power Company. The normally dry riverbed was transformed into a raging torrent, producing a rarely witnessed spectacle of falling water. The waterfall featured in this scene is Ladore Falls, and infamous Hawthorne's

Pool gets plenty of film time as well as the desperate boaters struggle to survive their ordeal. Visitors to Tallulah Gorge State Park can enjoy a bird's-eye view of this dramatic scene from a series of overlooks atop the high cliffs bordering Hawthorne's Pool.

Hawthorne's Pool and the sheer cliffs reaching to the northern rim of the gorge, site of several dramatic scenes from Deliverance. *The photo shows the scene with the bare minimum flow which was common in the years before Tallulah Gorge State Park was established.*

As recounted earlier in this publication, Hawthorne's Pool was the site of a tragic drowning in the early 1800s.

Note the final tongue of white water extending into the pool at the base of Ladore Falls, and the ruins of an early water diversion tunnel on the right.

THE DREAM BECOMES REALITY - TALLULAH GORGE BECOMES A STATE PARK

In the years after Tallulah dam was constructed, access to the gorge was over private property along a system of dangerous, unmaintained trails. The fragile ecosystem of the gorge was often abused by careless and destructive behavior of visitors, and injuries and deaths became commonplace. It often seemed that Tallulah Gorge was destined to be abused and mistreated.

Eighty years after Helen Dortch Longstreet led the great conservation battle to keep the Tallulah River running wild and free, at least a portion of her bold vision for a park came to reality when in 1993, Tallulah Gorge State Park was formed as a cooperative venture between the Georgia Department of Natural Resources and Georgia Power Company.

Nineteenth century visitors marvelled at the intricate beauty of Bridal Veil Falls. Modern-day visitors take their appreciation a step further.

As the twenty-first century dawns, Tallulah Gorge State Park provides one of the most dramatic natural experiences in Georgia's state park system. The Jane Hurt Yarn Interpretive Center provides a first-class educational experience detailing Tallulah Falls' rich history and complex ecological systems.

A vastly expanded and improved network of trails laces this 3,000+ acre park, providing access to many of the gorge's most beautiful recesses. Highlights include a dramatic stair system leading from both rims down to a breathtaking suspension bridge hanging nearly 100 feet above the river.

A photographer captures the resurrected might of Ladore Falls during an autumn whitewater release at Tallulah Gorge.

Though Mrs. Longstreet lost her valiant battle to halt construction of the dams, she no doubt would have been gratified to see Tallulah's wonderful waterfalls leaping from the rocky cliffs once again.

For eighty years, only a small amount of water flowed through the gorge, rendering Tallulah's legendary falls virtually lifeless. Shortly after the park was established a small culvert was inserted near the top of Tallulah dam to provide a constant minimum flow through the gorge. Though not dramatic, Tallulah's riverbed and legendary waterfalls were reenergized. In addition, scheduled "aesthetic" water releases further enhance the scenery and atmosphere of the gorge.

Waterfall watchers desiring the ultimate Tallulah experience should plan to be on hand on one of the select weekends (normally in early April and early November) when the flood gates atop Tallulah dam are opened to provide sufficient water levels for whitewater boating *in* the gorge. It is during these rare occasions that Tallulah's major waterfalls regain their legendary former personalities, providing visitors with a chance to see and hear why Tallulah Falls was once known as the "Niagara of the South."

In addition to the gorge itself, the park features a number of enticing destinations. As it nears its centennial, Tallulah Lake still draws crowds for fishing, paddling and swimming. A number of long trails have been developed which reach into the wilderness recesses of the park. Railroad buffs will love the "Shortline Trail," a paved multi-use pathway following a highly scenic portion of the old Tallulah Falls Railroad line.

Though perhaps not exactly as Mrs. Longstreet may have envisioned it over eighty years ago,

The park's dramatic suspension bridge crosses the gorge floor above the brink of mighty Hurricane Falls.

Tallulah Gorge seems to have finally found a much deserved niche under the watchful eye of the Georgia Department of Natural Resources.

The changes have been nothing less than dramatic. Just a decade ago visitors were forced to explore at their own peril, but much needed safeguards are now in place, protecting both humans and the fragile ecosystems of the gorge. Nearly a century ago, those who loved Tallulah Gorge for its wild and exquisite natural beauty were left to ponder its fate after the dams robbed it of its lifeblood. Today visitors are once again able to experience Tallulah Gorge much as it was before man interfered.

A boater is dwarfed by the mighty cliffs of the inner gorge just downstream of the whitewater put-in at Hurricane Falls.

TALLULAH FALLS AND TALLULAH GORGE - WHAT DOES THE FUTURE HOLD?

Following the damming of the gorge and the disastrous 1921 fire, Tallulah Falls settled into its new life as a sleepy mountain stop on the way to higher, cooler destinations further north. The gorge still featured trademark postcard scenery, but without the Tallulah River's lifeblood most spectators treated it simply as a curiosity, perhaps stopping alongside the highway for a quick peak before proceeding on their journeys.

The town survived the dramatic upheavals of the early 1900s, but only a handful of structures remained from its glory days. The Tallulah Falls Railroad continued to stop at the picturesque Tallulah Falls depot, but eventually the old TF carried only freight. The crowded excursion trains disappeared, replaced by efficient and convenient modern highways. The railroad disappeared completely in 1961, it too a victim of cheaper, more convenient modes of hauling freight. Though the old depot remained, it eventually began to appear out of place as the tracks and trestles of the railroad were dismantled and hauled away. As the various cuts and fills which designated the railroad's route began to become overgrown and fall into disrepair, the memory of the old line began to fade.

Life in Tallulah Falls continued at a slow pace for generations, but don't be fooled into believing that the town is dead. Today, Tallulah Falls School is a vibrant and growing educational institution where hundreds of young persons come to obtain a quality education. Tallulah Gorge State Park has become one of the crown jewels of the Georgia state park system, boasting of spectacular scenery and outstanding recreational and educational opportunities. Spectacular whitewater releases bring thousands of visitors to Tallulah once again, filling the gorge with thunderous spray and regenerating its spectacular beauty.

But what about the future? What will become of the once great town? While no one knows for certain, it is sure to involve growth and change.

Early 20th century postcard portrays a lazy summer scene on Tallulah Lake, much the same as what you might see today in the 21st century.

As the northeast Georgia mountains continue to attract visitors and residents alike, more and more people discover the beauty of the gorge and its elusive cascades. Events like the annual Tallulah Falls Whitewater Festival and Saturday night bluegrass in the summer months introduce more of Tallulah Falls' charms to the public. There's even renewed talk of an amphitheatre, perhaps fulfilling the vision of those who brought the great Wallenda to Tallulah Falls back in 1970.

Can Tallulah Falls ever recapture its prominent position of the late 1800s? Unlikely, considering the many obstacles that would have to be overcome. Though today's visitors won't be able to experience the grand hotels of yesteryear, they will be able to see and experience the gorge much like those who came here during the romantic days of the late 1800s. The town did indeed survive, and those who choose to linger today will be rewarded with a taste of what made Tallulah Falls Georgia's first great mountain resort well over a century ago.

A vintage postcard pictures a large group of boys posing atop a massive rock slab in the gorge years before the formation of the park.

Early visitors pose for a photographer at the Glenbrook Hotel's gazebo.

Print reproduced from a Currier & Ives lithograph featured on a 1973 calender produced by The Travelers Insurance Companies.

PHOTO CREDITS

page courtsey of

iii - Tallulah Falls School Museum
2 - George and Vickie Prater
5 - George and Vickie Prater
7 (top) - Georgia Department of Archives and History
7 (bottom) - Georgia Department of Archives and History
10 - Frances Causey, Gail Geary and Vera Claire Legg
11 (top) - George and Vickie Prater
11 (bottom) - George and Vickie Prater
12 - Georgia Department of Archives and History
13 - Frances Causey, Gail Geary and Vera Claire Legg
15 - Brian A. Boyd
20 - Tresa Dyer
21 - Georgia Department of Archives and History
22 - George and Vickie Prater
24 - John Kollock
25 - Georgia Department of Archives and History
26 - George and Vickie Prater
27 - Georgia Department of Archives and History
28 - R.D. Sharpless, from the collection of Frank Ardrey, Jr.
32 - Tallulah Falls School Museum
32 (bottom) - Georgia Department of Archives and History
33 - John Kollock
34 - George and Vickie Prater
35 - George and Vickie Prater
37 - Frances Causey, Gail Geary and Vera Claire Legg
38 - John Kollock
39 - John Kollock
42 - Georgia Department of Archives and History
43 - Georgia Power Corporate Archives

page courtsey of

44 - Frances Causey, Gail Geary and Vera Claire Legg
45 (top) - George and Vickie Prater
45 (bottom) - George and Vickie Prater
46 (top) - George and Vickie Prater
46 (bottom) - George and Vickie Prater
47 - George and Vickie Prater
49 - collection of Brian A. Boyd
51 - J.V. Michael Motes
52 - J.V. Michael Motes
53 - George and Vickie Prater
57 - Georgia Department of Natural Resources/Tallulah Gorge State Park
58 - Georgia Department of Natural Resources/Tallulah Gorge State Park
59 - Rabun Gap-Nacoochee School Archives
60 - George and Vickie Prater
61 (top) - J.V. Michael Motes
61 (bottom) - George and Vickie Prater
65 - George and Vickie Prater
66 (top) - Georgia Power Corporate Archives
66 (bottom) - Tallulah Falls School Museum
67 (top left) - George and Vickie Prater
67 (top right) - George and Vickie Prater
67 (bottom) - Georgia Department of Archives and History
68 - Georgia Power Corporate Archives
69 - Georgia Power Corporate Archives
70 - Georgia Power Corporate Archives
71 (top) - Georgia Power Corporate Archives

PHOTO CREDITS

page courtsey of

71 (bottom) - Frances Causey, Gail Geary and Vera Claire Legg
72 - Georgia Power Corporate Archives
74 - Foxfire Archives
78 - Tallulah Falls School Museum
79 - Tallulah Falls School Museum
80 (top) - Tallulah Falls School Mus.
80 (bottom) - George and Vickie Prater
81 - Tallulah Falls School Museum
82 - Georgia Power Corporate Archives
83 - John Kollock
84 (top) - Western Carolina University Library/Special Collections
84 (bottom) - Western Carolina University Library/Special Collections
85 - Western Carolina University Library/Special Collections
86 (top) - Western Carolina Univer sity Library/Special Collections
86 (bottom) - Western Carolina University Library/Special Collections
87 - Western Carolina University Library/Special Collections
88 (top) - George and Vickie Prater
88 (bottom left) - George and Vickie Prater
88 (bottom right) - George and Vickie Prater
89 (top) - George and Vickie Prater
89 (middle) - Western Carolina University Library/Special Collections
89 (bottom) - Western Carolina University Library/Special Collections
90 (top) - Tallulah Falls School Museum

page courtsey of

90 (bottom) - George and Vickie Prater
91 - collection of Brian A. Boyd
92 - collection of Brian A. Boyd
93 (top left) - collection of Brian A. Boyd
93 (top right) - collection of Brian A. Boyd
94 (top) - Georgia Department of Natural Resources/Tallulah Gorge State Park
94 (bottom) - collection of Brian A. Boyd
95 - Georgia Department of Natural Resources/Tallulah Gorge State Park
96 - Georgia Department of Natural Resources/Tallulah Gorge State Park
98 - Brian A. Boyd
99 - Brian A. Boyd
100 - Brian A. Boyd
101 - Brian A. Boyd
102 - Brian A. Boyd
104 - George and Vickie Prater
105 - George and Vickie Prater
106 - John Kollock
107 - Brian A. Boyd

cover photographs - (front): Tallulah Falls School Museum. (back cover): (top left) John Kollock; (top right): Frances Causey, Gail Geary, and Vera Claire Legg; (bottom left): Georgia Department of Archives and History.

Photographs from the Western Carolina University Library, Special Collections were taken by Mr. R.A. Romanes.

BIBLIOGRAPHY

Banner-Watchman, *Athens Banner-Watchman* and *Athens Daily Banner*, various issues, 1880s and 1890s.

Bartlett, Harry, "Fire At The Falls!," *North Georgia Journal*, Spring, 1993.

Calhoon, Margaret and Speno, Lynn, *Tallulah Falls*, Arcadia Publishing, Charleston, SC, 1998.

Coulter, E. Merton, "Tallulah Falls, Georgia's Natural Wonder, From Creation to Destruction," *Georgia Historical Quarterly*, XLVII (1963), 121-157, 249-275.

Georgia Department of Natural Resources, Tallulah Gorge State Park, miscellaneous archival papers and photographs.

Hancock, Carol Stevens, *The Light in the Mountains*, Commercial Printing Company, Toccoa, GA, 1975.

Kollock, John, *These Gentle Hills*, Copple House Books, Lakemont, GA, 1976.

Motes, Michael, "Aunt Fannie Smith, The Famous Hostess of Sinking Mountain," *Georgia Magazine*, August 1971, 16-18.

North Georgia Hydro Group, Georgia Power Company, 1987.

Reynolds, George P., *Foxfire 10*, Anchor Books, New York, 1993.

Ritchie, Andrew, *Sketches of Rabun County, 1819-1948*, Atlanta, Foote and Davies, 1948.

Saye, John, *The Life and Times of Tallulah...The Falls, The Gorge, The Town*, Tallulah Falls School, Tallulah Falls, GA, 1986.

INDEX

INDEX

INDEX

INDEX

ODDS 'N ENDS

1890s advertisements for Tallulah establishments-

Glenbrook Cottage

A Dreamland of Romance

Surrounded by bluegrass lawns, shaded by spreading virgin oaks, the breezes perfumed by incense of the flowering vine, cooled by the diamond spray from fountains midst the foliage, this "Home of Nature" offers the acme of comfort and attractions to the visitor. Come and judge for yourself. Come to Glenbrook.

Search high and low, where'er you will,
Seek down the dale, or on the hill,
You'll never find a fairer nook,
Than bonny, smiling chaste Glenbrook.

Mrs. M. A. Hunnicutt, Tallulah Falls, GA

J. Hamp Vickery W. J. Alford

"The Niagara of the South"

The Leading Bar and Wine Cellar of Tallulah

Where you will find at any time the -
- Best of drinks, either hot or ice cold
- Anyone who visits our place of business will find a cordial welcome and ample protection.
- Our prices are as cheap as the quality of the goods we keep will allow.

Call and be convinced.

NOTES